Empire
of Signs

BOOKS BY ROLAND BARTHES

A Barthes Reader
Camera Lucida
Critical Essays
The Eiffel Tower and Other Mythologies
Elements of Semiology
Empire of Signs
The Fashion System
The Grain of the Voice
Image-Music-Text
A Lover's Discourse
Michelet
Mythologies
New Critical Essays
On Racine
The Pleasure of the Text
The Responsibility of Forms
Roland Barthes
The Rustle of Language
Sade / Fourier / Loyola
The Semiotic Challenge
S / Z
Writing Degree Zero

Roland Barthes

Empire of Signs

TRANSLATED BY RICHARD HOWARD

HILL AND WANG
A DIVISION OF FARRAR, STRAUS AND GIROUX
NEW YORK

Hill and Wang
A division of Farrar, Straus and Giroux
18 West 18th Street, New York 10011

Printed in the United States of America
Originally published in 1970 by Editions d'Art Albert Skira S.A., Switzerland,
as *L'Empire des signes*
Published in 1982 in the United States by Hill and Wang
First paperback edition, 1983

The Library of Congress has cataloged the hardcover edition as follows:
Barthes, Roland.
    Empire of signs / Roland Barthes ; translated by Richard Howard.— 1st
American ed.
        p.   cm.
    Translation of: L'empire des signes.
    ISBN-13: 978-0-8090-4222-7
    ISBN-10: 0-8090-4222-3
    1. Japan—Civilization.   I. Title.

DS821 .B31713   1982
952—dc19

                                                                    82011868

Paperback ISBN-13: 978-0-374-52207-0
Paperback ISBN-10: 0-374-52207-3

Designed by Stephen Dyer

www.fsgbooks.com

39 40 38

To Maurice Pinguet

Contents

FARAWAY 3

THE UNKNOWN LANGUAGE 6

WITHOUT WORDS 9

WATER AND FLAKE 11

CHOPSTICKS 15

FOOD DECENTERED 19

THE INTERSTICE 24

PACHINKO 27

CENTER-CITY, EMPTY CENTER 30

NO ADDRESS 33

THE STATION 38

PACKAGES 43

THE THREE WRITINGS 48

ANIMATE/INANIMATE 58

INSIDE/OUTSIDE 61

BOWING 63

THE BREACH OF MEANING 69

EXEMPTION FROM MEANING 73

THE INCIDENT 77

SO 81

STATIONERY STORE 85

THE WRITTEN FACE 88

vii

MILLIONS OF BODIES   95
THE EYELID   99
THE WRITING OF VIOLENCE   103
THE CABINET OF SIGNS   107

Illustrations

2 The actor Kazuo Funaki

5 The character *Mu*, signifying "nothing," "emptiness," drawn by a student

21 Yoko Yayu (1702–83): Mushroom picking. Ink on paper
    When they hunt for mushrooms, the Japanese take with them a fern stem or, as in this painting, a wisp of straw, on which they string the mushrooms. Haiga painting, linked to the haiku
        He becomes greedy
        his eyes lowered
        on the mushrooms

31 Map of Tokyo, late eighteenth century

34 Map of the Shinjuku district, Tokyo: bars, restaurants, cinemas, department store (Isetan)

35 Orientation sketch

36 Orientation sketch on the back of a calling card

40-1 Sumi wrestlers

44 Sake kegs

ix

50-1 Shikidai gallery—Nijo Castle, Kyoto, built in 1603

52-3 Kabuki actor on stage and in private life

56 Gesture of a calligraphy master

64 On the Yokohama dock, from *Japon illustré* by Félicien Challaye, Paris, 1915

66-7 Offering a present, from *Japon illustré*

90 Press clipping from the newspaper *Kobe Shinbun*, and portrait of the actor Teturo Tanba

92-3 Last photographs of General Nogi and his wife, taken the day before their suicide in September 1912. From *Japon illustré*

100-1 Children in front of a puppet show, 1951

104-5 Student demonstration in Tokyo against the Vietnam War

109 The actor Kazuo Funaki

The text does not "gloss" the images, which do not "illustrate" the text. For me, each has been no more than the onset of a kind of visual uncertainty, analogous perhaps to that *loss of meaning* Zen calls a *satori*. Text and image, interlacing, seek to ensure the circulation and exchange of these signifiers: body, face, writing; and in them to read the retreat of signs.

*Empire
of Signs*

Faraway

If I want to imagine a fictive nation, I can give it an invented name, treat it declaratively as a novelistic object, create a new Garabagne, so as to compromise no real country by my fantasy (though it is then that fantasy itself I compromise by the signs of literature). I can also—though in no way claiming to represent or to analyze reality itself (these being the major gestures of Western discourse)—isolate somewhere in the world (*faraway*) a certain number of features (a term employed in linguistics), and out of these features deliberately form a system. It is this system which I shall call: Japan.

Hence Orient and Occident cannot be taken here as "realities" to be compared and contrasted historically, philosophically, culturally, politically. I am not lovingly gazing toward an Oriental essence—to me the Orient is a matter of indifference, merely providing a reserve of features whose manipulation—whose invented interplay—allows me to "entertain" the idea of an unheard-of symbolic system, one altogether detached from our own. What can be addressed, in the consideration of the Orient, are not other symbols, another metaphysics, another wisdom (though the latter might appear thoroughly desirable); it is the possibility of a difference, of a mutation, of a revolution in the propriety of symbolic

3

systems. Someday we must write the history of our own obscurity—manifest the density of our narcissism, tally down through the centuries the several appeals to difference we may have occasionally heard, the ideological recuperations which have infallibly followed and which consist in always acclimating our incognizance of Asia by means of certain known languages (the Orient of Voltaire, of the *Revue Asiatique*, of Pierre Loti, or of *Air France*). Today there are doubtless a thousand things to learn about the Orient: an enormous labor of *knowledge* is and will be necessary (its delay can only be the result of an ideological occultation); but it is also necessary that, leaving aside vast regions of darkness (capitalist Japan, American acculturation, technological development), a slender thread of light search out not other symbols but the very fissure of the symbolic. This fissure cannot appear on the level of cultural products: what is presented here does not appertain (or so it is hoped) to art, to Japanese urbanism, to Japanese cooking. The author has never, in any sense, photographed Japan. Rather, he has done the opposite: Japan has starred him with any number of "flashes"; or, better still, Japan has afforded him a situation of writing. This situation is the very one in which a certain disturbance of the person occurs, a subversion of earlier readings, a shock of meaning lacerated, extenuated to the point of its irreplaceable void, without the object's ever ceasing to be significant, desirable. Writing is after all, in its way, a *satori*: *satori* (the Zen occurrence) is a more or less powerful (though in no way formal) seism which causes knowledge, or the subject, to vacillate: it creates *an emptiness of language*. And it is also an emptiness of language which constitutes writing; it is from this emptiness that derive the features with which Zen, in the exemption from all meaning, writes gardens, gestures, houses, flower arrangements, faces, violence.

Mu, emptiness

The Unknown Language

The dream: to know a foreign (alien) language and yet not to understand it: to perceive the difference in it without that difference ever being recuperated by the superficial sociality of discourse, communication or vulgarity; to know, positively refracted in a new language, the impossibilities of our own; to learn the systematics of the inconceivable; to undo our own "reality" under the effect of other formulations, other syntaxes; to discover certain unsuspected positions of the subject in utterance, to displace the subject's topology; in a word, to descend into the untranslatable, to experience its shock without ever muffling it, until everything Occidental in us totters and the rights of the "father tongue" vacillate— that tongue which comes to us from our fathers and which makes us, in our turn, fathers and proprietors of a culture which, precisely, history transforms into "nature." We know that the chief concepts of Aristotelian philosophy have been somehow *constrained* by the principal articulations of the Greek language. How beneficial it would be, conversely, to gain a vision of the irreducible differences which a very remote language can, by glimmerings, suggest to us. One chapter by Sapir or Whorf on the Chinook, Nootka, Hopi languages, by Granet on Chinese, a friend's remark on Japanese opens up the whole fictive realm, of which only certain modern texts (but no novel) can afford a notion, permitting us to perceive a landscape which our speech (the speech we own) could under no circumstances either discover or divine.

Thus, in Japanese, the proliferation of functional suffixes and the complexity of enclitics suppose that the subject advances into utterance through certain precautions, repetitions, delays, and insistances whose final volume (we can no longer speak of a simple line of words) turns the subject, precisely, into a great envelope empty of speech, and not that dense kernel which is supposed to direct our sentences, from outside and from above, so that what seems to us an excess of subjectivity (Japanese, it is said, articulates impressions, not affidavits) is much more a way of diluting, of hemorrhaging the subject in a fragmented, particled language diffracted to emptiness. Or again this: like many languages, Japanese distinguishes animate (human and/or animal) from inanimate, notably on the level of its verbs *to be*; and the fictive characters introduced into a story (*once upon a time there was a king*) are assigned the form of the inanimate; whereas our whole art struggles to enforce the "life," the "reality" of fictive beings, the very structure of Japanese restores or confines these beings to their quality as *products*, signs cut off from the alibi referential par excellence: that of the living thing. Or again, in a still more radical way, since it is a matter of conceiving what our language does not conceive: how can we *imagine* a verb which is simultaneously without subject, without attribute, and yet transitive, such as for instance an act of knowledge without knowing subject and without known object? Yet it is this imagination which is required of us faced with the Hindu *dhyana*, origin of the Chinese *ch'an* and the Japanese *zen*, which we obviously cannot translate by *meditation* without restoring to it both

7

subject and god: drive them out, they return, and it is our language they ride on. These phenomena and many others convince us how absurd it is to try to contest our society without ever conceiving the very limits of the language by which (instrumental relation) we claim to contest it: it is trying to destroy the wolf by lodging comfortably in its gullet. Such exercises of an aberrant grammar would at least have the advantage of casting suspicion on the very ideology of our speech.

Without Words

The murmuring mass of an unknown language constitutes a delicious protection, envelops the foreigner (provided the country is not hostile to him) in an auditory film which halts at his ears all the alienations of the mother tongue: the regional and social origins of whoever is speaking, his degree of culture, of intelligence, of taste, the image by which he constitutes himself as a person and which he asks you to recognize. Hence, in foreign countries, what a respite! Here I am protected against stupidity, vulgarity, vanity, worldliness, nationality, normality. The unknown language, of which I nonetheless grasp the respiration, the emotive aeration, in a word the pure significance, forms around me, as I move, a faint vertigo, sweeping me into its artificial emptiness, which is consummated only for me: I live in the interstice, delivered from any fulfilled meaning. *How did you deal with the language?* Subtext: *How did you satisfy that vital need of communication?* Or more precisely, an ideological assertion masked by the practical interrogation: *there is no communication except in speech.*

Now it happens that in this country (Japan) the empire of signifiers is so immense, so in excess of speech, that the exchange of signs remains of a fascinating richness, mobility, and subtlety, despite the opacity of the language, sometimes even as a consequence of that opacity. The reason for this is that in Japan the body exists, acts, shows itself, gives itself, without hysteria, without narcissism, but according to a pure —though subtly discontinuous—erotic project. It is not the voice (with which we identify the "rights" of the person) which communicates (communicates what? our—necessarily beautiful—soul? our sincerity? our prestige?), but the whole body (eyes, smile, hair, gestures, clothing) which sustains with you a sort of babble that the perfect domination of the codes strips of all regressive, infantile character. To make a date (by gestures, drawings on paper, proper names) may take an hour, but during that hour, for a message which would be abolished in an instant if it were to be spoken (simultaneously quite essential and quite insignificant), it is the other's entire body which has been known, savored, received, and which has displayed (to no real purpose) its own narrative, its own text.

Water and Flake

The dinner tray seems a picture of the most delicate order: it is a frame containing, against a dark background, various objects (bowls, boxes, saucers, chopsticks, tiny piles of food, a little gray ginger, a few shreds of orange vegetable, a background of brown sauce), and since these containers and these bits of food are slight in quantity but numerous, it might be said that these trays fulfill the definition of painting which, according to Piero della Francesca, "is merely a demonstration of surfaces and bodies becoming ever smaller or larger according to their term." However, such an order, delicious when it appears, is destined to be undone, recomposed according to the very rhythm of eating; what was a motionless tableau at the start becomes a workbench or chessboard, the space not of seeing but of doing— of *praxis* or play; the painting was actually only a palette (a work surface), with which you are going to play in the course of your meal, taking up here a pinch of vegetables, there of rice, and over there of condiment, here a sip of soup, according to a free alternation, in the manner of a (specifically Japanese) graphic artist set down in front of a series of pots who, at one and the same time, knows and hesitates; so that, without being denied or diminished (no question of an indifference with regard to food—an attitude that is always *moral*), eating remains stamped with a kind of work or play which bears less on the transformation of the primary substance (an object proper to the *kitchen* and to *cuisine*; but Japanese food is rarely cooked, the foodstuffs arrive in their natural state on the tray; the only operation they have actually undergone is to be cut up) than on the shifting and somehow inspired assemblage of elements whose order of selection is fixed by no protocol (you can alternate a sip of soup, a mouthful of rice, a pinch of vegetables): the entire *praxis* of alimentation being in the composition, by composing your choices, you yourself make what it is you eat; the dish is no longer a reified product, whose preparation is, among us, modestly distanced in time and in space (meals elaborated in advance behind the partition of a kitchen, secret room where *everything is permitted*, provided the product emerges from it all the more composed, embellished, embalmed, shellacked). Whence the *living* (which does not mean *natural*) character of this food, which in each season seems to fulfill the poet's wish: *"Oh, to celebrate the spring by exquisite cookeries . . ."*

From painting, Japanese food also takes the least immediately visual quality, the quality most deeply engaged in the body (attached to the weight and the labor of the hand which draws or covers) and which is not color but *touch.* Cooked rice (whose absolutely special identity is attested to by a special name, which is not that of raw rice) can be defined only by a contradiction of substance; it is at once cohesive and detachable; its substantial destination is the fragment, the clump, the volatile conglomerate; it is the only element of weight in all of Japanese alimentation (antinomic to the Chinese); it is what sinks, in opposition to what floats; it constitutes in the picture a compact whiteness, granular (contrary to that of our bread) and yet friable: what comes

le rendez-vous

Ouvrez un guide de voyage : vous y
trouverez d'ordinaire un petit lexique,
mais ce lexique portera bizarrement sur
les choses ennuyeuses et inutiles : la douane,
la poste, l'hôtel, le coiffeur, le médecin,
les prix. Cependant, qu'est-ce que
voyager ? Rencontrer. Le seul lexique
important est celui du rendez-vous.

The rendezvous

Open a travel guide: usually you will find a brief lexicon which
strangely enough concerns only certain boring and useless things:
customs, mail, the hotel, the barber, the doctor, prices. Yet what is
traveling? Meetings. The only lexicon that counts is the one which
refers to the rendezvous.

to the table, dense and stuck together, comes undone at a touch of the chopsticks, though without ever scattering, as if division occurred only to produce still another irreducible cohesion; it is this measured (incomplete) defection which, beyond (or short of) the food, is offered to be consumed. In the same way—but at the other extremity of substances—Japanese soup (this word *soup* is unduly thick, and our French word *potage* suggests the *pension de famille*) adds a touch of clarity to the alimentary interplay. For us, in France, a clear soup is a poor soup; but here the lightness of the bouillon, fluid as water, the soybean dust or minced green beans drifting within it, the rarity of the two or three solids (shreds of what appears to be grass, filaments of vegetable, fragments of fish) which divide as they float in this little quantity of water give the idea of a clear density, of a nutrivity without grease, of an elixir all the more comforting in that it is pure: something aquatic (rather than aqueous), something delicately marine suggests a spring, a profound vitality. Hence Japanese food establishes itself within a reduced system of substance (from the clear to the divisible), in a shimmer of the signifier: these are the elementary characters of the writing, established upon a kind of vacillation of language, and indeed this is what Japanese food appears to be: a written food, tributary to the gestures of division and selection which inscribe the foodstuff, not on the meal tray (nothing to do with photographed food, the gaudy compositions of our women's magazines), but in a profound space which hierarchizes man, table, and universe. For writing is precisely that act which unites in the same labor what could not be apprehended together in the mere flat space of representation.

Chopsticks

At the Floating Market in Bangkok, each vendor sits in a tiny motionless canoe, selling minuscule quantities of food: seeds, a few eggs, bananas, coconuts, mangoes, pimentos (not to speak of the Unnamable). From himself to his merchandise, including his vessel, everything is *small*. Occidental food, heaped up, dignified, swollen to the majestic, linked to a certain operation of prestige, always tends toward the heavy, the grand, the abundant, the copious; the Oriental follows the converse movement, and tends toward the infinitesimal: the cucumber's future is not its accumulation or its thickening, but its division, its tenuous dispersal, as this haiku puts it:

> *Cucumber slices*
> *The juice runs*
> *Drawing spider legs*

There is a convergence of the tiny and the esculent: things are not only small in order to be eaten, but are also comestible in order to fulfill their essence, which is smallness. The harmony between Oriental food and chopsticks cannot be merely functional, instrumental; the foodstuffs are cut up so they can be grasped by the sticks, but also the chopsticks exist because the foodstuffs are cut into small pieces; one and the same movement, one and the same form transcends the substance and its utensil: division.

Chopsticks have other functions besides carrying the food from the plate to the mouth (indeed, that is the least pertinent one, since it is also the function of fingers and forks), and these functions are specifically theirs. First of all, a chopstick—as its shape sufficiently indicates—has a deictic function: it points to the food, designates the fragment, brings into existence by the very gesture of choice, which is the index; but thereby, instead of ingestion following a kind of mechanical sequence, in which one would be limited to swallowing little by little the parts of one and the same dish, the chopstick, designating what it selects (and thus selecting there and then *this* and not *that*), introduces into the use of food not an order but a caprice, a certain indolence: in any case, an intelligent and no longer mechanical operation. Another function of the two chopsticks together, that of pinching the fragment of food (and no longer of piercing it, as our forks do); to *pinch*, moreover, is too strong a word, too aggressive (the word of sly little girls, of surgeons, of seamstresses, of sensitive natures); for the foodstuff never undergoes a pressure greater than is precisely necessary to raise and carry it; in the gesture of chopsticks, further softened by their substance—wood or lacquer—there is something maternal, the same precisely measured care taken in moving a child: a force (in the operative sense of the word), no longer a pulsion; here we have a whole demeanor with regard to food; this is seen clearly in the cook's long chopsticks, which serve not for eating but for preparing foodstuffs: the instrument never pierces, cuts, or slits, never wounds but only selects, turns, shifts. For the chopsticks (third function), in order to divide, must separate, part, peck, instead of cutting

rendez vray   rendezvous
yakusoku   yakuso ku

tous les deux   both
tutaritomo   tutaritomo

où?   where?
doko ni?   doko ni?

quand?   when?
itsu?   itsu?

and piercing, in the manner of our implements; they never violate the foodstuff: either they gradually unravel it (in the case of vegetables) or else prod it into separate pieces (in the case of fish, eels), thereby rediscovering the natural fissures of the substance (in this, much closer to the primitive finger than to the knife). Finally, and this is perhaps their loveliest function, the chopsticks *transfer* the food, either crossed like two hands, a support and no longer a pincers, they slide under the clump of rice and raise it to the diner's mouth, or (by an age-old gesture of the whole Orient) they push the alimentary snow from bowl to lips in the manner of a scoop. In all these functions, in all the gestures they imply, chopsticks are the converse of our knife (and of its predatory substitute, the fork): they are the alimentary instrument which refuses to cut, to pierce, to mutilate, to trip (very limited gestures, relegated to the preparation of the food for cooking: the fish seller who skins the still-living eel for us exorcises once and for all, in a preliminary sacrifice, the murder of food); by chopsticks, food becomes no longer a prey to which one does violence (meat, flesh over which one does battle), but a substance harmoniously transferred; they transform the previously divided substance into bird food and rice into a flow of milk; maternal, they tirelessly perform the gesture which creates the mouthful, leaving to our alimentary manners, armed with pikes and knives, that of predation.

Food Decentered

Sukiyaki is a stew whose every element can be known and recognized, since it is made in front of you, on your table, without interruption while you are eating it. The raw substances (but peeled, washed, already garbed in an aesthetic nakedness, shiny, bright-colored, harmonious as a spring garment: *"color, delicacy, touch, effect, harmony, relish—everything can be found here,"* Diderot would say) are gathered together and brought to the table on a tray: it is the very essence of the market that comes to you, its freshness, its naturalness, its diversity, and even its classification, which turns the simple substance into the promise of an event: recrudescence of appetite attached to this compound object which is the market product, at once nature and merchandise, commercial nature, accessible to popular possession: edible leaves, vegetables, angel hair, creamy squares of bean curd, raw egg yolk, red meat and white sugar (an alliance infinitely more exotic, more fascinating or more disgusting, because visual, than the simple *sweet / sour* of Chinese food, which is always cooked and in which sugar is not seen except in the caramelized luster of certain "lacquered" dishes), all these raw substances, initially allied, composed as in a Dutch painting of which they retain the linear contour, the elastic firmness of the brushwork, and the bright-colored finish (impossible to say if this is the consequence of the substance of things, the lighting of the scene, the unguent that coats the painting, or the museum illumination), gradually transferred to the big pot in which they stew before your eyes, losing their colors, their shapes, and their discontinuity, softening, denaturing, becoming that *roux* which is the essential color of the sauce; while you select, with your chopsticks, certain fragments of this new-made stew, other raw substances will be added to replace them. Over this process presides an assistant who, placed a little behind you and armed with long chopsticks, alternately feeds the pot and the conversation: it is an entire minor odyssey of food you are experiencing through your eyes: you are attending the Twilight of the Raw.

This Rawness, we know, is the tutelary divinity of Japanese food: to it everything is dedicated, and if Japanese cooking is always performed in front of the eventual diner (a fundamental feature of this cuisine), this is probably because it is important to consecrate by spectacle the death of what is being honored. What is being honored in what the French call *crudité* or rawness (a term we use, oddly enough, in the singular to denote the sexuality of language and in the plural to name the external, abnormal, and somewhat taboo part of our menus) is apparently not, as with us, an inner essence of the foodstuff, the sanguinary plethora (blood being the symbol of strength and death) by which we assimilate vital energy by transmigration (for us, rawness is a *strong state* of food, as is metonymically shown by the intensive seasoning we impose on our *steak tartare*). Japanese rawness is essentially visual; it denotes a certain colored state of the flesh or vegetable substance (it being understood that color is never exhausted by a catalogue of tints, but refers to a whole tactility of substance; thus *sashimi* exhibits not so

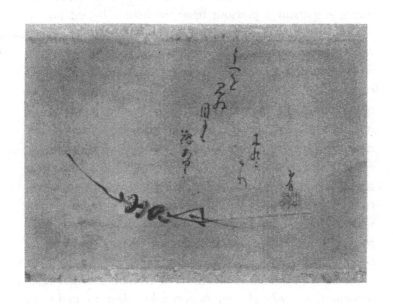

Where does the writing begin?
Where does the painting begin?

much colors as resistances: those which vary the flesh of raw fish, causing it to pass, from one end of the tray to the other, through the stations of the soggy, the fibrous, the elastic, the compact, the rough, the slippery). Entirely visual (conceived, concerted, manipulated for sight, and even for a painter's eye), food thereby says that it is not *deep*: the edible substance is without a precious heart, without a buried power, without a vital secret: no Japanese dish is endowed with a *center* (the alimentary center implied in the West by the rite which consists of arranging the meal, of surrounding or covering the article of food); here everything is the ornament of another ornament: first of all because on the table, on the tray, food is never anything but a collection of fragments, none of which appears privileged by an order of ingestion; to eat is not to respect a menu (an itinerary of dishes), but to select, with a light touch of the chopsticks, sometimes one color, sometimes another, depending on a kind of inspiration which appears in its slowness as the detached, indirect accompaniment of the conversation (which itself may be extremely silent); and then because this food—and this is its originality —unites in a single time that of its fabrication and that of its consumption: *sukiyaki*, an interminable dish to make, to consume, and, one might say, to "converse," not by any technical difficulty but because it is in its nature to exhaust itself in the course of its cooking, and consequently *to repeat itself*—*sukiyaki* has nothing *marked* about it except its beginning (that tray painted with foodstuffs brought to the table); once "started," it no longer has moments or distinctive sites: it becomes decentered, like an uninterrupted text.

Le rendez-vous

ici
koko ni

ce soir
komban

aujourd'hui
kyo

à quelle heure ?
nan ji ni ?

demain
ashata

quatre heures
yo ji

The meeting

here	tonight
koko ni	komban
today	what time?
kyo	nan ji ni?
tomorrow	four o'clock
ashata	yo ji

The Interstice

The cook (who cooks nothing at all) takes a living eel, sticks a long pin into its head, and scrapes it, skins it. This scene, so rapid and wet (rather than bloody), of minor cruelty will conclude in *lace*. The eel (or the piece of vegetable, of shellfish), crystallized in grease, like the Branch of Salzburg, is reduced to a tiny clump of emptiness, a collection of perforations: here the foodstuff joins the dream of a paradox: that of a purely interstitial object, all the more provocative in that this emptiness is produced in order to provide nourishment (occasionally the foodstuff is constructed in a ball, like a wad of air).

Tempura is stripped of the meaning we traditionally attach to fried food, which is heaviness. Here flour recovers its essence as scattered flower, diluted so lightly that it forms a milk and not a paste; taken up by the oil, this golden milk is so fragile that it covers the piece of food imperfectly, reveals here a pink of shrimp, there a green of pepper, a brown of eggplant, thus depriving the fry of what constitutes our fritter, which is its sheath, its envelope, its density. The oil (but is this oil—are we really dealing with the maternal substance, *the oily*?), immediately soaked up by the paper napkin on which you are served your *tempura* in a little wicker basket—the oil is dry, utterly unrelated to the lu-

24

bricant with which the Mediterranean and the Near East cover their cooking and their pastry; it loses a contradiction which marks our foodstuffs cooked in oil or grease, which is to burn without heating; this cold burning of the fat body is here replaced by a quality which seems denied to all fried food: freshness. The freshness which circulates in *tempura* through the floury lace, tang of the toughest and of the most fragile among foodstuffs, fish and vegetables—this freshness, which is both that of what is intact and that of what is refreshing, is indeed that of the oil: *tempura* restaurants are classified according to the degree of freshness of the oil they use: the most expensive ones use new oil, which is ultimately sold to less pretentious restaurants, and so forth; it is not the food-stuff the diner pays for, or even its freshness (still less the status of the premises or the service), it is the virginity of its cooking.

Sometimes the piece of *tempura* is in stages: the fry out-lines (better than: envelops) a pepper, itself chambered inside; what matters here is that the foodstuff be constituted as a piece, a fragment (fundamental state of the Japanese cuisine, in which blending—in a sauce, a cream, a crust—is unknown), not only by its preparation but also and especially by its immersion in a substance fluid as water, cohesive as grease, out of which emerges a fragment completed, sepa-rated, named and yet entirely perforated; but the contour is so light that it becomes abstract: the foodstuff has for its envelope nothing but time, the time (itself extremely tenu-ous, moreover) which has solidified it. It is said that *tempura* is a dish of Christian (Portuguese) origin: it is the food of lent (*tempora*); but refined by the Japanese techniques of cancellation and exemption, it is the nutriment of another time: not of a rite of fasting and expiation, but of a kind of meditation, as much spectacular as alimentary (since *tempura* is prepared before your eyes), around an item we ourselves select, lacking anything better (and perhaps by reason of our thematic ruts), on the side of the light, the aerial, of the instantaneous, the fragile, the transparent, the crisp, the trifling, but whose real name would be *the interstice* without specific edges, or again: the empty sign.

As a matter of fact, we must return to the young artist who makes lace out of fish and peppers. If he prepares our food *in front of us*, conducting, from gesture to gesture, from place to place, the eel from the breeding pond to the white paper which, in conclusion, will receive it entirely perforated, it is not (only) in order to make us witnesses to the extreme precision and purity of his cuisine; it is because his activity is literally graphic: he inscribes the foodstuff in the substance; his stall is arranged like a calligrapher's table; he touches the substances like the graphic artist (especially if he is Japanese) who alternates pots, brushes, inkstone, water, paper; he thereby accomplishes, in the racket of the restaurant and the chaos of shouted orders, a hierarchized arrangement, not of time but of tenses (those of a grammar of *tempura*), makes visible the entire gamut of practices, recites the foodstuff not as a finished merchandise, whose perfection alone would have value (as is the case with our dishes), but as a product whose meaning is not final but progressive, exhausted, so to speak, when its production has ended: it is you who eat, but it is he who has played, who has written, who has produced.

Pachinko

Pachinko is a slot machine. At the counter you buy a little stock of what look like ball bearings; then, in front of the machine (a kind of vertical panel), with one hand you stuff each ball into a hole, while with the other, by turning a flipper, you propel the ball through a series of baffles; if your initial dispatch is just right (neither too strong nor too weak), the propelled ball releases a rain of more balls, which fall into your hand, and you have only to start over again—unless you choose to exchange your winnings for an absurd reward (a candy bar, an orange, a pack of cigarettes). Pachinko parlors are extremely numerous, and always full of a varied clientele (young people, women, students in black tunics, middle-aged men in business suits). It is said that pachinko turnovers are equal (or even superior) to those of all the department stores in Japan (which is certainly saying a good deal).

The pachinko is a collective and solitary game. The machines are set up in long rows; each player standing in front of his panel plays for himself, without looking at his neighbor, whom he nonetheless brushes with his elbow. You hear only the balls whirring through their channels (the rate of insertion is very rapid); the parlor is a hive or a factory—the players seem to be working on an assembly

line. The imperious meaning of the scene is that of a delib-
erate, absorbing labor; never an idle or casual or playful
attitude, none of that theatrical unconcern of our Western
players lounging in leisurely groups around a pinball machine
and quite conscious of producing for the other patrons of the
café the image of an expert and disillusioned god. As for the
art of playing the game, it too differs from that of our machines. For the Western player, once the ball is propelled, the
main thing is to correct its trajectory as it falls back down (by
giving little nudges to the machine); for the Japanese player,
everything is determined in the initial dispatch, everything
depends on the force the thumb imparts to the flipper; the
adroitness is immediate, definitive, it alone accounts for the
talent of the player, who can correct chance only in advance
and in a single movement; or more exactly: the propulsion
of the ball is at best only delicately constrained or halted
(but not at all directed) by the hand of the player, who with
a single movement moves and observes: this hand is therefore
that of an artist (in the Japanese fashion), for whom the
(graphic) feature is a "controlled accident." Pachinko reproduces, in short, on the mechanical level, precisely the principle of painting *alla prima*, which insists that the line be
drawn in a single movement, once and for all, and that by
reason of the very quality of the paper and the ink, it can
never be corrected; in the same way the ball, once propelled,
cannot be deviated (it would be an outrageous piece of
boorishness to shake the machine, as our Western sports do):
its path is predetermined by the sole flash of its impetus.

What is the use of this art? to organize a nutritive circuit.
The Western machine sustains a symbolism of penetration:
the point is to possess, by a well-placed thrust, the pinup girl
who, all lit up on the panel of the machine, allures and waits.
In pachinko, no sex (in Japan—in that country I am calling

Japan—sexuality is in sex, not elsewhere; in the United States, it is the contrary; sex is everywhere, except in sexuality). The machines are mangers, lined up in rows; the player, with an abrupt gesture, renewed so rapidly that it seems uninterrupted, feeds the machine with his metal marbles; he stuffs them in, the way you would stuff a goose; from time to time the machine, filled to capacity, releases its diarrhea of marbles; for a few yen, the player is symbolically spattered with money. Here we understand the seriousness of a game which counters the constipated parsimony of salaries, the constriction of capitalist wealth, with the voluptuous debacle of silver balls, which, all of a sudden, fill the player's hand.

Center-City, Empty Center

Quadrangular, reticulated cities (Los Angeles, for instance) are said to produce a profound uneasiness: they offend our synesthetic sentiment of the City, which requires that any urban space have a center to go to, to return from, a complete site to dream of and in relation to which to advance or retreat; in a word, to invent oneself. For many reasons (historical, economic, religious, military), the West has understood this law only too well: all its cities are concentric; but also, in accord with the very movement of Western metaphysics, for which every center is the site of truth, the center of our cities is always *full*: a marked site, it is here that the values of civilization are gathered and condensed: spirituality (churches), power (offices), money (banks), merchandise (department stores), language (agoras: cafés and promenades): to go downtown or to the center-city is to encounter the social "truth," to participate in the proud plenitude of "reality."

The city I am talking about (Tokyo) offers this precious paradox: it does possess a center, but this center is empty. The entire city turns around a site both forbidden and indifferent, a residence concealed beneath foliage, protected by moats, inhabited by an emperor who is never seen, which is to say, literally, by no one knows who. Daily, in their rapid, ener-

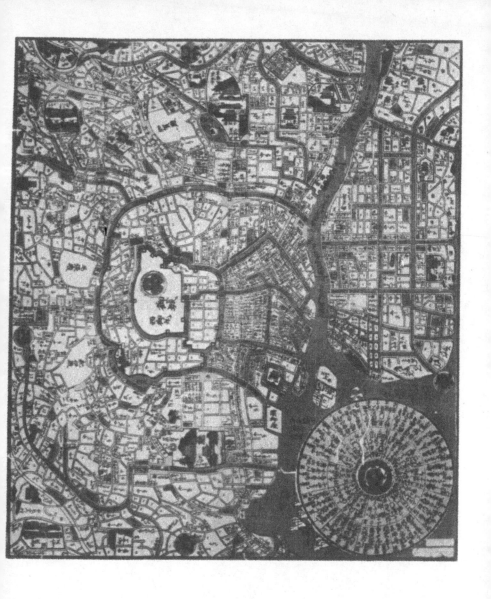

The City is an ideogram:
the Text continues

getic, bullet-like trajectories, the taxis avoid this circle, whose low crest, the visible form of invisibility, hides the sacred "nothing." One of the two most powerful cities of modernity is thereby built around an opaque ring of walls, streams, roofs, and trees whose own center is no more than an evaporated notion, subsisting here, not in order to irradiate power, but to give to the entire urban movement the support of its central emptiness, forcing the traffic to make a perpetual detour. In this manner, we are told, the system of the imaginary is spread circularly, by detours and returns the length of an empty subject.

No Address

The streets of this city have no names. There is of course a written address, but it has only a postal value, it refers to a plan (by districts and by blocks, in no way geometric), knowledge of which is accessible to the postman, not to the visitor: the largest city in the world is practically unclassified, the spaces which compose it in detail are unnamed. This domiciliary obliteration seems inconvenient to those (like us) who have been used to asserting that the most practical is always the most rational (a principle by virtue of which the best urban toponymy would be that of numbered streets, as in the United States or in Kyoto, a Chinese city). Tokyo meanwhile reminds us that the rational is merely one system among others. For there to be a mastery of the real (in this case, the reality of addresses), it suffices that there be a system, even if this system is apparently illogical, uselessly complicated, curiously disparate: a good *bricolage* can not only *work* for a very long time, as we know; it can also satisfy millions of inhabitants inured, furthermore, to all the perfections of technological civilization.

Anonymity is compensated for by a certain number of expedients (at least this is how they look to us), whose combination forms a system. One can figure out the address by a (written or printed) schema of orientation, a kind of geographical summary which situates the domicile starting from a known landmark; a train station, for instance. (The inhabitants excel in these impromptu drawings, where we see being sketched, right on the scrap of paper, a street, an apartment house, a canal, a railroad line, a shop sign, making the exchange of addresses into a delicate communication in which a life of the body, an art of the graphic gesture recurs: it is always enjoyable to watch someone write, all the more so to watch someone draw: from each occasion when someone has given me an address in this way, I retain the gesture of my interlocutor reversing his pencil to rub out, with the eraser at its other end, the excessive curve of an avenue, the intersection of a viaduct; though the eraser is an object contrary to the graphic tradition of Japan, this gesture still

Address book

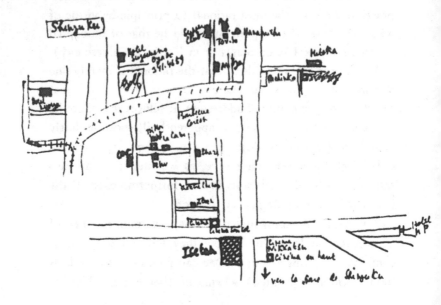

34

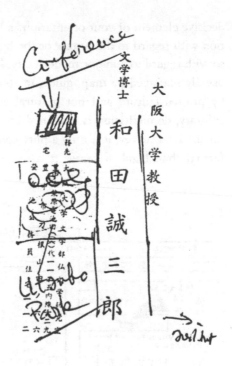

produced something peaceful, something caressing and certain, as if, even in this trivial action, the body "labored with more reserve than the mind," according to the precept of the actor Zeami; the fabrication of the address greatly prevailed over the address itself, and, fascinated, I could have hoped it would take hours to give me that address.) You can also, provided you already know where you are going, direct your taxi yourself, from street to street. And finally, you can request the driver to let himself be guided by the remote visitor to whose house you are going, by means of one of those huge red telephones installed in front of almost every shop in the street. All this makes the visual experience a decisive element of your orientation: a banal enough proposition with regard to the jungle or the bush, but one much less so with regard to a major modern city, knowledge of which is usually managed by map, guide, telephone book; in a word, by printed culture and not gestural practice. Here, on the contrary, domiciliation is sustained by no abstraction; except for the land survey, it is only a pure contingency: much more factual than legal, it ceases to assert the conjunction of an

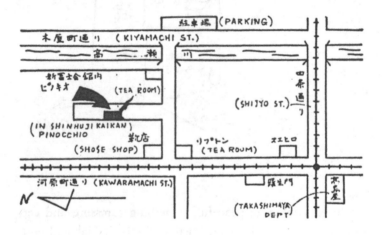

identity and a property. This city can be known only by an activity of an ethnographic kind: you must orient yourself in it not by book, by address, but by walking, by sight, by habit, by experience; here every discovery is intense and fragile, it can be repeated or recovered only by memory of the trace it has left in you: to visit a place for the first time is thereby to begin to write it: the address not being written, it must establish its own writing.

Le rendez-vous

peut-être   fatigué
tabun   tsukareta

impossible   je veux dormir
deki nai   netai

The rendezvous

maybe   tired
tabun   tsukareta

impossible   I want to sleep
deki nai   netai

The Station

In this enormous city, really an urban territory, the name of each district is distinct, known, placed on the rather empty map (the streets are not named) like a news flash; it assumes that strongly signifying identity which Proust, in his fashion, has explored in his Place Names. If the neighborhood is quite limited, dense, contained, terminated beneath its name, it is because it has a center, but this center is spiritually empty: usually it is a station.

The station, a vast organism which houses the big trains, the urban trains, the subway, a department store, and a whole underground commerce—the station gives the district this landmark which, according to certain urbanists, permits the city to signify, to be read. The Japanese station is crossed by a thousand functional trajectories, from the journey to the purchase, from the garment to food: a train can open onto a shoe stall. Dedicated to commerce, to transition, to departure, and yet kept in a unique structure, the station (moreover, is that what this new complex should be called?) is stripped of that sacred character which ordinarily qualifies the major landmarks of our cities: cathedrals, town halls, historical monuments. Here the landmark is entirely prosaic; no doubt the market is also a central site of the Western city; but in Tokyo merchandise is in a sense undone by the station's instability: an incessant departure thwarts its concentration; one might say that it is only the preparatory substance of the package and that the package itself is only the pass, the ticket which permits departure.

Thus each district is collected in the void of its station, an empty point-of-affluence of all its occupations and its pleasures. This day, I decide to go to one neighborhood or another, without any goal but a kind of prolonged perception of its name. I know that at Ueno I will find a station filled on its ground level with young skiers, but whose underground floors, extensive as a city, lined with foodstalls, with bars, populated with bums, with travelers sleeping, talking, eating on the very floor of these sordid corridors, finally fulfills the novelistic essence of *the lower depths*. Quite close by—but on another day—will be another populous district: in the commercial streets of Asakusa (no cars), arched by paper cherry blossoms, are sold brand-new clothes, comfortable and very cheap: heavy leather jackets (nothing delinquent about them), gloves edged with black fur, very long wool scarves which one throws over one shoulder as would village children coming home from school, leather caps, all the gleaming and woolly gear of the good workman who must dress warmly, corroborated by the comfort of the huge steaming basins in which simmers a noodle soup. And on the other side of the imperial ring (empty, as we recall) is still another populous neighborhood: Ikebukuro, workers and farmers, harsh and friendly as a big mongrel dog. All these districts produce different races, distinct bodies, a familiarity new each time. To cross the city (or to penetrate its depth, for underground there are whole networks of bars, shops to which you sometimes gain access by a simple entryway, so that, once through this narrow door, you discover, dense and sumptuous, the black India of commerce and pleasure) is to travel from the

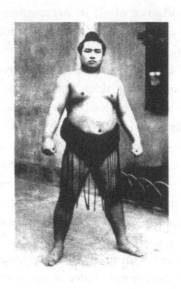

These wrestlers constitute a caste; they live apart, wear their hair long, and eat a ritual diet. The match lasts only an instant: the time it takes to let the other mass fall. No crisis, no drama, no exhaustion, in a word, no sport: the sign of a certain hefting, not the erethism of conflict

top of Japan to the bottom, to superimpose on its topography the writing of its faces. Thus each name echoes, evoking the idea of a village, furnished with a population as individual as that of a tribe, whose immense city would be the bush. This sound of the place is that of history; for the signifying name here is not a memory but an anamnesis, as if all Ueno, all Asakusa came to me from this old haiku (written by Basho in the seventeenth century):

A cloud of blossoming cherry trees:
The bell. —Ueno's?
Asakusa's?

Packages

If the bouquets, the objects, the trees, the faces, the gardens, and the texts—if the things and manners of Japan seem diminutive to us (our mythology exalts the big, the vast, the broad, the open), this is not by reason of their size, it is because every object, every gesture, even the most free, the most mobile, seems *framed*. The miniature does not derive from the dimension but from a kind of precision which the thing observes in delimiting itself, stopping, finishing. This precision has nothing specifically reasonable or moral about it: the thing is not *distinct* in a puritanical manner (by cleanness, frankness, or objectivity) but rather by hallucinatory or fantasmal addition (analogous to the vision resulting from hashish, according to Baudelaire) or by an excision which removes the flourish of meaning from the object and severs from its presence, from its position in the world, any *tergiversation*. Yet this frame is invisible: the Japanese thing is not outlined, illuminated; it is not formed of a strong contour, a drawing which would "fill out" the color, the shadow, the texture; around it, there is: *nothing*, an empty space which renders it matte (and therefore to our eyes: reduced, diminished, small).

It is as if the object frustrates, in a manner at once unexpected and pondered, the space in which it is always

43

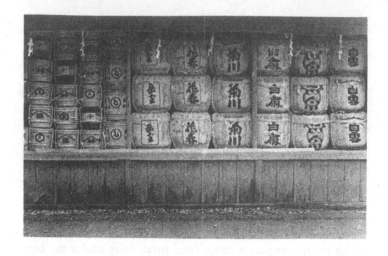

located. For example: the room keeps certain written limits, these are the floor mats, the flat windows, the walls papered with bamboo paper (pure image of the surface), from which it is impossible to distinguish the sliding doors; here everything is *line*, as if the room were written with a single stroke of the brush. Yet, by a secondary arrangement, this rigor is in its turn baffled: the partitions are fragile, breakable, the walls slide, the furnishings can be whisked away, so that you rediscover in the Japanese room that "fantasy" (of dressing, notably) thanks to which every Japanese foils—without taking the trouble or creating the theater to subvert it—the conformism of his context. Or again: in a Japanese flower arrangement, "rigorously constructed" (according to the language of Western aesthetic), and whatever the symbolic intentions of this construction as set forth in every guide to Japan and in every art book on the *Ikebana*, what is produced is the circulation of air, of which flowers, leaves, branches (words that are far too botanical) are only the walls, the corridors, the baffles, delicately drawn according to the notion of a *rarity* which we dissociate, for our part, from nature, as if only profusion *proved* the natural; the Japanese bouquet has a volume; unknown masterpiece, as dreamed of by Frenhofer, Balzac's hero who wanted the viewer to be able to pass behind the painted figure, you can move your body into the interstice of its branches, into the space of its stature, not in order to *read* it (to read its symbolism) but to follow the trajectory of the hand which has written it: a true writing, since it produces a volume and since, forbidding our reading to be the simple decoding of a message (however loftily symbolic), it permits this reading to repeat the course of the writing's labor. Or lastly (and especially): without even regarding as emblematic the famous set of Japanese boxes, one inside the other down to emptiness, you can already see a true semantic meditation in the merest Japanese package. Geometric, rigorously drawn, and yet always signed some-where with an asymmetrical fold or knot, by the care, the very technique of its making, the interplay of cardboard, wood, paper, ribbon, it is no longer the temporary accessory of the object to be transported, but itself becomes an object; the envelope, in itself, is consecrated as a precious though gratuitous thing; the package is a thought; thus, in a vaguely pornographic magazine, the image of a naked Japanese boy, tied up very neatly like a sausage: the sadistic intent (paraded much more than achieved) is naïvely—or ironically—absorbed in the practice, not of a passivity, but of an extreme art: that of the package, of *fastening* . . .

Yet, by its very perfection, this envelope, often repeated (you can be unwrapping a package forever), postpones the discovery of the object it contains—one which is often in-significant, for it is precisely a specialty of the Japanese package that the triviality of the thing be disproportionate to the luxury of the envelope: a sweet, a bit of sugared bean paste, a vulgar "souvenir" (as Japan is unfortunately so expert at producing) are wrapped with as much sumptuousness as a jewel. It is as if, then, the box were the object of the gift, not what it contains: hordes of schoolboys, on a day's outing, bring back to their parents a splendid package containing no one knows what, as if they had gone very far away and this was an occasion for them to devote themselves in troops to the ecstasy of the package. Thus the box acts the sign: as envelope, screen, mask, it is *worth* what it conceals, protects, and yet designates: it *puts off*, if we can take this expression in French—*donner le change*—in its double meaning, monetary and psychological; but the very thing it encloses and signifies is for a very long time put off until later, as if the package's function were not to protect in space but to postpone in time; it is in the envelope that the labor of the confection (of the making) seems to be invested, but thereby the object loses its existence, becomes a mirage: from envelope to envelope, the signified flees, and when you finally have it (there is always a little *something* in the package), it appears insignificant, laughable, vile: the pleasure, field of the signifier, has been taken: the package is not empty, but emptied: to find the object which is in the package or the signified which is in the sign is to discard it: what the Japanese carry, with a formicant energy, are actually empty signs. For there is in Japan a profusion of what we might call: the instruments of transport; they are of all kinds, of all shapes, of all substances: packages, pouches, sacks, valises, linen wrappings (the *fujo*, a peasant handkerchief or scarf in which the thing is wrapped), every citizen in the street has some sort of bundle, an empty sign, energetically protected, vigorously transported, as if the finish, the framing, the hallucinatory outline which establishes the Japanese object destined it to a generalized transport. The richness of the thing and the profundity of meaning are discharged only at the price of a triple quality imposed on all fabricated objects: that they be precise, mobile, and empty.

The Three Writings

Bunraku dolls are from three to five feet high. They are little men or women with movable hands, feet, and mouths; each doll is moved by three quite visible men who surround it, support it, accompany it; the leader works the upper part of the doll and its right arm; his face is apparent, smooth, bright, impassive, cold as "a white onion that has just been washed" (Basho); the two helpers wear black, a piece of cloth conceals their faces; one, in gloves but with the thumb showing, holds a huge pair of shears with which he moves the doll's left arm and hand; the other, crawling, supports the body, and is responsible for the doll's walking. These men proceed along a shallow trench which leaves their bodies visible. The setting is behind them, as in our theater. To one side, a dais receives the musicians and the speakers; their role is to *express* the text (as one might squeeze a fruit); this text is half spoken, half sung, punctuated with loud plectrum strokes by the samisen players, so that it is both measured and impassioned, with violence and artifice. Sweating and motionless, the speakers are seated behind little lecterns on which is set the huge script which they vocalize and whose vertical characters you can glimpse from a distance, when they turn a page of their libretto; a triangle of stiff canvas, attached to their shoulders like a bat's wing, frames their face, which is subject to all the throes of the voice.

Bunraku thus practices three separate writings, which it offers to be read simultaneously in three sites of the spectacle: the puppet, the manipulator, the vociferant: the effected gesture, the effective gesture, and the vocal gesture. The voice: real stake of our modernity, special substance of language, which we try to make triumph everywhere. Quite the contrary, *Bunraku* has a *limited* notion of the voice; it does not suppress the voice, but assigns it a very clearly defined, essentially trivial function. In the speaker's voice are gathered together: exaggerated declamation, tremolos, a falsetto tonality, broken intonations, tears, paroxysms of rage, of supplication, of astonishment, indecent pathos, the whole cuisine of emotion, openly elaborated on the level of that internal, visceral body of which the larynx is the mediating muscle. Yet this excess is given only within the very code of excess: the voice moves only through several discontinuous signs of the tempestuous; expelled from a motionless body, triangulated by the garment, connected to the text which, from its desk, guides it, strictly punctuated by the slightly out-of-phase (and thereby even impertinent) strokes of the samisen player, the vocal substance remains written, discontinuous, coded, subject to an irony (if we may strip this word of any caustic meaning); hence, what the voice ultimately externalizes is not what it carries (the "sentiments") but itself, its own prostitution; the signifier cunningly does nothing but turn itself inside out, like a glove.

Without being eliminated (which would be a way of censuring it, i.e., of designating its importance), the voice is thus set aside (scenically, the speakers occupy a lateral dais). *Bunraku* gives the voice a counterpoise, or better still, a countermove: that of gesture. This gesture is double: emotive

Turn the image upside down:

nothing more, nothing else, nothing

The Oriental transvestite does not copy Woman but signifies her:
not bogged down in the model, but detached from its signified;
Femininity is presented to read, not to see: translation, not trans-
gression; the sign shifts from the great female role to the fifty-year-
old paterfamilias: he is the same man, but where does the
metaphor begin?

gesture on the level of the doll (audiences weep at the mistress-doll's suicide), transitive action on the level of the manipulators. In our theatrical art, the actor pretends to act, but his actions are never anything but gestures: on stage, nothing but theater, yet a theater ashamed of itself. Whereas *Bunraku* (this is its definition) separates action from gesture: it shows the gesture, lets the action be seen, exhibits simultaneously the art and the labor, reserving for each its own writing. The voice (and there is then no risk in letting it attain the excessive regions of its range) is accompanied by a vast volume of silence, in which are inscribed, with all the more finesse, other features, other writings. And here there occurs an unheard-of effect: remote from the voice and almost without mimicry, these silent writings, one transitive, the other gestural, produce an exaltation as special, perhaps, as the intellectual hyperesthesia attributed to certain drugs. Language being not *purified* (*Bunraku* is quite unconcerned with ascesis), but one might say *collected* to one side of the acting, all the importunate substances of Western theater are dissolved: emotion no longer floods, no longer submerges, but becomes a reading, the stereotypes disappear without, for all that, the spectacle collapsing into originality, "lucky finds." All this connects, of course, with the alienation effect Brecht recommends. That distance, regarded among us as impossible, useless, or absurd, and eagerly abandoned, though Brecht very specifically located it at the center of his revolutionary dramaturgy (and the former no doubt explains the latter), that distance is made explicable by *Bunraku*, which allows us to see how it can function: by the discontinuity of the codes, by this caesura imposed on the various features of representation, so that the copy elaborated on the stage is not destroyed but somehow broken, striated, withdrawn from that metonymic contagion of voice and gesture, body and soul, which entraps our actors.

A total spectacle but a divided one, *Bunraku* of course excludes improvisation: to return to spontaneity would be to return to the stereotypes which constitute our "depth." As Brecht had seen, here *citation* rules, the sliver of writing, the fragment of code, for none of the action's promoters can account in his own person for what he is never alone to write. As in the modern text, the interweaving of codes, references, discrete assertions, anthological gestures multiplies the written line, not by virtue of some metaphysical appeal, but by the interaction of a *combinatoire* which opens out into the entire space of the theater: what is begun by one is continued by the next, without interval.

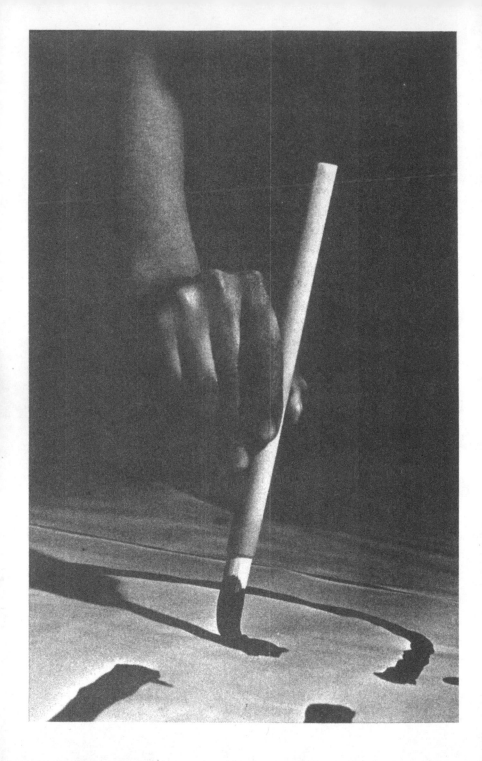

Writing, then, rises from the plane of inscription because it
results from a recoil and a non-regardable discrepancy (not
from a face-to-face encounter; inciting from the first not
what is seen but what can be traced) which divides the
support into corridors as though to recall the plural void in
which it is achieved—it is merely *detached* on the surface,
it proceeds to weave itself there, delegated from depths
which are not deep toward the surface, which is no longer a
surface but a fiber *written from beneath vertical to its upper
surface* (the brush stands straight up in the palm)—the
ideogram thereby returning to the column—tube or ladder
—and taking its place there as a complex bar released by
the monosyllable in the field of the voice: this column can
be called an "empty wrist," in which first appears as a
"unique feature" the breath which passes through the
hollowed arm, the perfect operation necessarily being that of
the "concealed point" or of the "absence of traces."

Philippe Sollers, *On Materialism*, 1969

Animate / Inanimate

Concerned with a basic antinomy, that of *animate / inanimate, Bunraku* jeopardizes it, eliminates it without advantage for either of its terms. In the West, the puppet (Punch, for instance) is supposed to offer the actor the mirror of his contrary; it animates the inanimate, but the better to manifest its degradation, the unworthiness of its inertia; caricature of "life," it thereby affirms life's *moral* limits and claims to confine beauty, truth, emotion within the living body of the actor, who, however, makes this body a lie. *Bunraku*, however, does not sign the actor, it gets rid of him for us. How? Precisely by a certain idea of the human body, which the inanimate substance here controls with infinitely more rigor and inspiration than the animate body (endowed with a "soul"). The Western (naturalist) actor is never beautiful; his body seeks to be a physiological essence and not a plastic one: it is a collection of organs, a musculature of passions, each of whose devices (voices, faces, gestures) is subject to a kind of gymnastic exercise; but by a strictly bourgeois reversal, although the actor's body is constructed according to a division of passional essences, it borrows from physiology the alibi of an organic unity, that of "life": it is the actor who is the puppet here, despite the connective tissue of his acting, of which the model is not the caress but only visceral "truth."

The basis of our theatrical art is indeed much less the illusion of reality than the illusion of totality: periodically, from the Greek *choreia* to bourgeois opera, we conceive lyric art as the simultaneity of several expressions (acted, sung, mimed), whose origin is unique, indivisible. This origin is the body, and the totality insisted on has for its model the body's organic unity: Western spectacle is anthropomorphic; in it, gesture and speech (not to mention song) form a single tissue, conglomerated and lubrified like a single muscle which makes expression function but never divides it up: the unity of movement and voice produces *the one* who acts; in other words, it is in this unity that the "person" of the character is constituted, i.e., the actor. As a matter of fact, beneath his "living" and "natural" externals, the Western actor preserves the division of his body and, thereby, the nourishment of our fantasies: here the voice, there the gaze, there again the figure are eroticized, as so many fragments of the body, as so many fetishes. The Western puppet, too (as is quite apparent in our Punch and Judy), is a fantasmal by-product: as a reduction, as a grim reflection whose adherence to the human order is ceaselessly recalled by a caricatural simulation, the puppet does not live as a total body, totally alive, but as a rigid portion of the actor from whom it has emanated; as an automaton, it is still a piece of movement, jerk, shock, essence of discontinuity, decomposed projection of the body's gestures; finally, as a doll, reminiscence of the bit of rag, of the genital bandage, it is indeed the phallic "little thing" ("das Kleine") fallen from the body to become a fetish.

It may well be that the Japanese puppet keeps something of this fantasmal origin; but the art of *Bunraku* imprints a different meaning on it; *Bunraku* does not aim at "animating" an inanimate object so as to make a piece of the body, a scrap of a man, "alive," while retaining its vocation as a "part"; it is not the simulation of the body that it seeks but, so to speak, its sensuous abstraction. Everything which we attribute to the total body and which is denied to our actors under cover of an organic, "living" unity, the little man of *Bunraku* recuperates and expresses without any deception: fragility, discretion, sumptuousness, unheard-of nuance, the abandonment of all triviality, the melodic phrasing of gestures, in short the very qualities which the dreams of ancient theology granted to the redeemed body, i.e., impassivity, clarity, agility, subtlety, this is what the *Bunraku* achieves, this is how it converts the body-as-fetish into the lovable body, this is how it rejects the antinomy of *animate / inanimate* and dismisses the concept which is hidden behind all animation of matter and which is, quite simply, "the soul."

Inside / Outside

Take the Western theater of the last few centuries; its function is essentially to manifest what is supposed to be secret ("feelings," "situations," "conflicts"), while concealing the very artifice of such manifestation (machinery, painting, makeup, the sources of light). The stage since the Renaissance is the space of this lie: here everything occurs in an interior surreptitiously open, surprised, spied on, savored by a spectator crouching in the shadows. This space is theological—it is the space of Sin: on one side, in a light which he pretends to ignore, the actor, i.e., the gesture and the word; on the other, in the darkness, the public, i.e., consciousness.

Bunraku does not directly subvert the relation of house and stage (though Japanese theaters are infinitely less confined, less enclosed, less weighed down than ours); what it transforms, more profoundly, is the motor link which proceeds from character to actor and which is always conceived, in the West, as the expressive means of an inwardness. We must recall that the agents of the spectacle, in *Bunraku*, are at once visible and impassive: the men in black busy themselves around the doll, but without any affectation of skill or of discretion and, one might say, without any paraded demagogy; silent, swift, elegant, their actions are eminently transitive, operative, tinged with that mixture of strength and subtlety which marks the Japanese repertoire of gestures and which is a kind of aesthetic envelope of effectiveness; as for the master, his head is uncovered; smooth, bare, without makeup, which accords him a civil (not a theatrical) distinction, his face is offered to the spectators to read; but what is carefully, preciously given to be read is that there is nothing there to read; here again we come to that exemption of meaning (that exemption *from* meaning as well) which we Westerners can barely understand, since, for us, to attack meaning is to hide or to invert it, but never to "absent" it. With *Bunraku*, the sources of the theater are exposed in their emptiness. What is expelled from the stage is hysteria, i.e., theater itself; and what is put in its place is the action necessary to the production of the spectacle: work is substituted for inwardness.

Hence it is futile to wonder, as certain Europeans do, if the spectator can ever forget the presence of the manipulators. *Bunraku* practices neither the occultation nor the emphatic manifestation of its means; hence it rids the actor's manifestation of any whiff of the sacred and abolishes the metaphysical link the West cannot help establishing between body and soul, cause and effect, motor and machine, agent and actor, Destiny and man, God and creature: if the manipulator is not hidden, why—and how—would you make him into a God? In *Bunraku*, the puppet has no strings. No more strings, hence no more metaphor, no more Fate; since the puppet no longer apes the creature, man is no longer a puppet in the divinity's hands, the *inside* no longer commands the *outside*.

Bowing

Why, in the West, is politeness regarded with suspicion? Why does courtesy pass for a distance (if not an evasion, in fact) or a hypocrisy? Why is an "informal" relation (as we so greedily say) more desirable than a coded one?

Occidental impoliteness is based on a certain mythology of the "person." Topologically, Western man is reputed to be double, composed of a social, factitious, false "outside" and of a personal, authentic "inside" (the site of divine communication). According to this schema, the human "person" is that site filled by nature (or by divinity, or by guilt), girdled, closed by a social envelope which is anything but highly regarded: the polite gesture (when it is postulated) is the sign of respect exchanged from one plenitude to the other, across the worldly limit (i.e., in spite and by the intermediary of this limit). However, as soon as the "inside" of the person is judged respectable, it is logical to recognize this person more suitably by denying all interest to his worldly envelope: hence it is the supposedly frank, brutal, naked relation, stripped (it is thought) of all signaletics, indifferent to any intermediary code, which will best respect the other's individual value: to be impolite is to be true—so speaks (logically enough) our Western morality. For if there is indeed a human "person" (dense, emphatic, centered, sacred), it is

doubtless this person which in an initial movement we claim to "salute" (with the head, the lips, the body); but my own person, inevitably entering into conflict with the other's plenitude, can gain recognition only by rejecting all mediation of the factitious and by affirming the integrity (highly ambiguous, this word: physical and moral) of its "inside"; and in a second impulse, I shall reduce my salute, I shall pretend to make it natural, spontaneous, disincumbered, purified of any code: I shall be scarcely affable, or affable according to an apparently invented fantasy, like the Princess of Parma (in Proust) signaling the breadth of her income and the height of her rank (i.e., her way of being "full" of things and of constituting herself a person), not by a distant stiffness of manner, but by the willed "simplicity" of her manners: how simple I am, how affable I am, how frank I am, how much I am *someone* is what Occidental impoliteness says.

The other politeness, by the scrupulosity of its codes, the distinct graphism of its gestures, and even when it seems to us exaggeratedly respectful (i.e., to our eyes, "humiliating") because we read it, in our manner, according to a metaphysics of the person—this politeness is a certain exercise of the void (as we might expect within a strong code but one signifying "nothing"). Two bodies bow very low before one another (arms, knees, head always remaining in a decreed place), according to subtly coded degrees of depth. Or again (on an old image): in order to give a present, I bow down, virtually to the level of the floor, and to answer me, my partner does the same: one and the same low line, that of

Who is saluting whom?

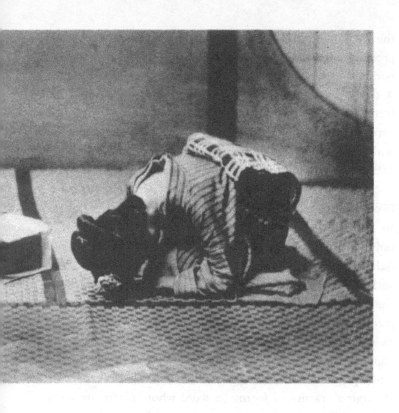

The gift is alone:
it is touched
neither by generosity
nor by gratitude,
the soul does not contaminate it

the ground, joins the giver, the recipient, and the stake of the protocol, a box which may well contain nothing—or virtually nothing; a graphic form (inscribed in the space of the room) is thereby given to the act of exchange, in which, by this form, is erased any greediness (the gift remains suspended between two disappearances). The salutation here can be withdrawn from any humiliation or any vanity, because it literally salutes *no one*; it is not the sign of a communication —closely watched, condescending and precautionary—between two autarchies, two personal empires (each ruling over its Ego, the little realm of which it holds the "key"); it is only the feature of a network of forms in which nothing is halted, knotted, profound. *Who is saluting whom?* Only such a question justifies the salutation, inclines it to the bow, the obeisance, and glorifies thereby not meaning but the inscription of meaning, and gives to a posture which we read as excessive the very reserve of a gesture from which any signified is inconceivably absent. *The Form is Empty*, says— and repeats—a Buddhist aphorism. This is what is expressed, through a practice of forms (a word whose plastic meaning and worldly meaning are here indissociable), by the politeness of the salutation, the bowing of two bodies which inscribe but do not prostrate themselves. Our ways of speaking are very vicious, for if I say that in that country politeness is a religion, I let it be understood that there is something sacred in it; the expression should be canted so as to suggest that religion there is merely a politeness, or better still, that religion has been replaced by politeness.

The Breach of Meaning

The haiku has this rather fantasmagorical property: that we always suppose we ourselves can write such things easily. We tell ourselves: what could be more accessible to spontaneous writing than this (by Buson):

> *It is evening, in autumn,*
> *All I can think of*
> *Is my parents.*

The haiku wakens desire: how many Western readers have dreamed of strolling through life, notebook in hand, jotting down "impressions" whose brevity would guarantee their perfection, whose simplicity would attest to their profundity (by virtue of a double myth, one classical, which makes concision a proof of art, the other romantic, which attributes a premium of truth to improvisation). While being quite intelligible, the haiku means nothing, and it is by this double condition that it seems open to meaning in a particularly available, serviceable way—the way of a polite host who lets you make yourself at home with all your preferences, your values, your symbols intact; the haiku's "absence" (we say as much of a distracted mind as of a landlord off on a journey) suggests subornation, a breach, in short the major covetousness, that of meaning. This precious, vital meaning, desirable as fortune (chance and money), the haiku, being without metrical constraints (in our translations), seems to afford in profusion, cheaply and made to order; in the haiku, one might say, symbol, metaphor, and moral cost almost nothing: scarcely a few words, an image, a sentiment—where our literature ordinarily requires a poem, a development or (in the genres of brevity) a chiseled thought; in short, a long rhetorical labor. Hence the haiku seems to give the West certain rights which its own literature denies it, and certain commodities which are parsimoniously granted. You are entitled, says the haiku, to be trivial, short, ordinary; enclose what you see, what you feel, in a slender horizon of words, and you will be interesting; you yourself (and starting from yourself) are entitled to establish your own notability; your sentence, whatever it may be, will enunciate a moral, will liberate a symbol, you will be profound: at the least possible cost, your writing will be *filled*.

The West moistens everything with meaning, like an authoritarian religion which imposes baptism on entire peoples; the objects of language (made out of speech) are obviously *de jure* converts: the first meaning of the system summons, metonymically, the second meaning of discourse, and this summons has the value of a universal obligation. We have two ways of sparing discourse the infamy of non-meaning (non-sense), and we systematically subject utterance (in a desperate filling-in of any nullity which might reveal the emptiness of language) to one or the other of these *significations* (or active fabrications of signs): symbol and reasoning, metaphor and syllogism. The haiku, whose propositions are always simple, commonplace, in a word *acceptable* (as we say in linguistics), is attracted into one or the other of these two empires of meaning. Since it is a "poem," we assign it to that part of the general code of sentiments called "poetic emotion" (for us, Poetry is ordinarily the signifier of the "diffuse," of the "ineffable," of the "sensitive," it is the class of impressions which are unclassifiable); we speak of "concentrated emotion," of "sincere notation of a privileged moment," and above all of "silence" (silence being for us the sign of language's fulfillment). If one of their poets (Joko) writes:

> How many people
> Have crossed the Seta bridge
> Through the autumn rain!

we perceive the image of fleeting time. If another (Basho) writes:

> I come by the mountain path.
> Ah! this is exquisite!
> A violet!

it is because he has encountered a Buddhist hermit, the "flower of virtue"; and so on. Not one feature fails to be invested by the Western commentator with a symbolic charge. Or again, we seek at all costs to construe the haiku's tercet (its three verses of five, seven, and five syllables) as a syllogistic design in three tenses (rise, suspense, conclusion):

> The old pond:
> A frog jumps in:
> Oh! the sound of the water.

(in this singular syllogism, inclusion is achieved by force: in order to be contained in it, the minor premise must leap into the major). Of course, if we renounce metaphor or syllogism, commentary would become impossible: to speak of the haiku would be purely and simply to repeat it. Which is what one commentator of Basho does, quite innocently:

> Already four o'clock ...
> I have got up nine times
> To admire the moon.

"The moon is so lovely," he says, "that the poet gets up repeatedly to contemplate it at his window." Deciphering, normalizing, or tautological, the ways of interpretation, intended in the West to *pierce* meaning, i.e., to get into it by breaking and entering—and not to shake it, to make it fall like the tooth of that ruminant-of-the-absurd which the Zen apprentice must be, confronting his *koan*—cannot help failing the haiku; for the work of reading which is attached to it is to suspend language, not to provoke it: an enterprise whose difficulty and necessity Basho himself, the master of the haiku, seemed to recognize:

> How admirable he is
> Who does not think "Life is ephemeral"
> when he sees a flash of lightning!

Exemption from Meaning

The whole of Zen wages a war against the prevarication of meaning. We know that Buddhism baffles the fatal course of any assertion (or of any negation) by recommending that one never be caught up in the four following propositions: *this is A—this is not A—this is both A and not-A—this is neither A nor not-A.* Now this quadruple possibility corresponds to the perfect paradigm as our structural linguistics has framed it (*A—not-A—neither A nor not-A* [zero degree]—*A and not-A* [complex degree]); in other words, the Buddhist way is precisely that of the obstructed meaning: the very arcanum of signification, that is, the paradigm, is rendered *impossible.* When the Sixth Patriarch gives his instructions concerning the *mondo,* a question-and-answer exercise, he recommends, in order to confuse the paradigmatic functioning more completely, as soon as a term is posited, to shift toward its adverse term (*"If, questioning you, someone interrogates you about non-being, answer with being. If you are questioned about the ordinary man, answer by speaking about the master, etc."*), so as to make the mockery of the paradigm and the mechanical character of meaning all the more apparent. What is aimed at (by a mental technique whose precision, patience, refinement, and learning attest to how difficult Oriental thought regards the

peremption of meaning), what is aimed at is the establish-
ment of the sign, i.e., classification (*maya*); constrained to
the classification *par excellence*, that of language, the haiku
functions at least with a view to obtaining a *flat* language
which nothing grounds (as is infallible in our poetry) on
superimposed layers of meaning, what we might call the
"lamination" of symbols. When we are told that it was the
noise of the frog which wakened Basho to the truth of Zén,
we can understand (thought this is still too Western a way
of speaking) that Basho discovered in this noise, not of
course the motif of an "illumination," of a symbolic hyperesthesia, but rather an end of language: there is a moment
when language ceases (a moment obtained by dint of many
exercises), and it is this echoless breach which institutes at
once the truth of Zen and the form—brief and empty—of
the haiku. The denial of "development" is radical here, for it
is not a question of halting language on a heavy, full, profound, mystical silence, or even on an emptiness of the soul
which would be open to divine communication (Zen knows
no God); what is posited must develop neither in discourse
nor in the end of discourse: what is posited is *matte*, and all
that one can do with it is to scrutinize it; this is what is
recommended to the apprentice who is working on a *koan*
(or anecdote proposed to him by his master): not to solve it,
as if it had a meaning, nor even to perceive its absurdity
(which is still a meaning), but to ruminate it "until the
tooth falls out." All of Zen, of which the haiku is merely the
literary branch, thus appears as an enormous praxis destined
to *halt language*, to jam that kind of internal radiophony
continually *sending* in us, even in our sleep (perhaps this is
the reason the apprentices are sometimes kept from falling
asleep), to empty out, to stupefy, to dry up the soul's in-
coercible babble; and perhaps what Zen calls *satori*, which

74

Westerners can translate only by certain vaguely Christian words (*illumination, revelation, intuition*), is no more than a panic suspension of language, the blank which erases in us the reign of the Codes, the breach of that internal recitation which constitutes our person; and if this state of *a-language* is a liberation, it is because, for the Buddhist experiment, the proliferation of secondary thoughts (the thought of thought), or what might be called the infinite supplement of supernumerary signifieds—a circle of which language itself is the depository and the model—appears as a jamming: it is on the contrary the *abolition* of secondary thought which breaks the vicious infinity of language. In all these experiments, apparently, it is not a matter of crushing language beneath the mystic silence of the ineffable, but of *measuring* it, of halting that verbal top which sweeps into its gyration the obsessional play of symbolic substitutions. In short, it is the symbol as semantic operation which is attacked.

In the haiku, the limitation of language is the object of a concern which is inconceivable to us, for it is not a question of being concise (i.e., shortening the signifier without diminishing the density of the signified) but on the contrary of acting on the very root of meaning, so that this meaning will not melt, run, internalize, become implicit, disconnect, divagate into the infinity of metaphors, into the spheres of the symbol. The brevity of the haiku is not formal; the haiku is not a rich thought reduced to a brief form, but a brief event which immediately finds its proper form. The *measurement* of language is what the Westerner is most unfit for: not that his utterance is too long or too short, but all his rhetoric obliges him to make signifier and signified disproportionate, either by "diluting" the latter beneath the garrulous waves of the former, or by "deepening" form toward the implicit regions of content. The haiku's accuracy (which is not at all an exact depiction of reality, but an adequation of signifier and signified, a suppression of margins, smudges, and interstices which usually exceed or perforate the semantic relation), this accuracy obviously has something musical about it (a music of meanings and not necessarily of sounds): the haiku has the purity, the sphericality, and the very emptiness of a note of music; perhaps that is why it is spoken twice, in echo; to speak this exquisite language only once would be to attach a meaning to surprise, to effect, to the suddenness of perfection; to speak it many times would postulate that meaning is to be discovered in it, would simulate profundity; between the two, neither singular nor profound, the echo merely draws a line under the nullity of meaning.

The Incident

Western art transforms the "impression" into description. The haiku never describes; its art is counter-descriptive, to the degree that each state of the thing is immediately, stubbornly, victoriously converted into a fragile essence of appearance: a literally "untenable" moment in which the thing, though being already only language, will become speech, will pass from one language to another and constitute itself as the memory of this future, thereby anterior. For in the haiku, it is not only the event proper which predominates:

> *(I saw the first snow:*
> *That morning I forgot*
> *To wash my face.)*

but even what seems to us to have a vocation as painting, as a miniature picture—the sort so numerous in Japanese art —such as this haiku by Shiki:

> *With a bull on board*
> *A little boat crosses the river*
> *Through the evening rain.*

becomes or is only a kind of absolute accent (as is given to each thing, trivial or not, in Zen), a faint plication by which is creased, with a rapid touch, the page of life, the silk of language. Description, a Western genre, has its spiritual equivalent in contemplation, the methodical inventory of the attributive forms of the divinity or of the episodes of evangelical narrative (in Ignatius Loyola, the exercise of contemplation is essentially descriptive); the haiku, on the contrary, articulated around a metaphysics without subject and without god, corresponds to the Buddhist *Mu*, to the Zen *satori*, which is not at all the illuminative descent of God, but "awakening to the fact," apprehension of the thing as event and not as substance, attaining to that anterior shore of language, contiguous to the (altogether retrospective, reconstituted) *matt*eness of the adventure (what happens to language, rather than to the subject).

The number and the dispersion of haikus on the one hand, the brevity and closure of each one on the other, seem to divide, to classify the world to infinity, to constitute a space of pure fragments, a dust of events which nothing, by a kind of escheat of signification, can or should coagulate, construct, direct, terminate. This is because the haiku's time is without subject: reading has no other *self* than all the haikus of which this *self*, by infinite refraction, is never anything but the site of reading; according to an image proposed by the Hua-yen doctrine, one might say that the collective body of all haikus is a network of jewels in which each jewel reflects all the others and so on, to infinity, without there ever being a center to grasp, a primary core of irradiation (for us, the clearest image of this ricochet effect without motor and without check, of this play of reflections without origin, would be that of the dictionary, in which a word can only be defined by other words). In the West, the mirror is an essentially narcissistic object: man conceives a mirror only in order to look at himself in it; but in the Orient, apparently, the mirror is empty; it is the symbol of the very emptiness of symbols (*"The mind of the perfect man,"* says one Tao master, *"is like a mirror. It grasps nothing but repulses nothing. It receives but does not retain"*): the mirror intercepts only other mirrors, and this infinite reflection is emptiness itself (which, as we know, is form). Hence the haiku reminds us of what has never happened to us; in it we *recognize* a repetition without origin, an event without cause, a memory without person, a language without moorings.

What I am saying here about the haiku I might also say about everything which *happens* when one travels in that country I am calling Japan. For there, in the street, in a bar, in a shop, in a train, something always *happens*. This something—which is etymologically an adventure—is of an infinitesimal order: it is an incongruity of clothing, an anachronism of culture, a freedom of behavior, an illogicality of itinerary, etc. To count up these events would be a Sisyphean enterprise, for they glisten only at the moment when one *reads* them, in the lively writing of the street, and the Westerner will be able to utter them spontaneously only by charging them with the very meaning of his distance: he would in fact have to make haiku out of them, a language which is denied us. What one can add is that these infinitesimal adventures (of which the accumulation, in the course of a day, provokes a kind of erotic intoxication) never have anything picturesque about them (the Japanese picturesque is indifferent to us, for it is detached from what constitutes the very specialty of Japan, which is its modernity), or anything novelistic (never lending themselves to the chatter which would make them into narratives or descriptions); what they offer to be *read* (I am, in that country, a reader, not a visitor) is the rectitude of the line, the stroke, without wake, without margin, without vibration; so many tiny demeanors (from garment to smile), which among us, as a result of the Westerner's inveterate narcissism, are only the signs of a swollen assurance, become, among the Japanese, mere ways of passing, of tracing some unexpected thing in the street: for the gesture's sureness and independence never refer back to an affirmation of the self (to a "self-sufficiency") but only to a graphic mode of existing; so that the spectacle of the Japanese street (or more generally of the public place), exciting as the product of an age-old aesthetic, from which all vulgarity has been decanted, never depends on a theatricality (a hysteria) of bodies, but, once more, on that writing *alla prima*, in which sketch and regret, calculation and correction are equally impossible, because the line, the tracing, freed from the advantageous image the scriptor would give of himself, does not express but simply *causes to exist*. "*When you walk*, says one Zen master, "*be content to walk. When you are seated, be content to be seated. But, above all, don't wriggle!*": this is what, in their way, all seem to be telling me—the young bicyclist carrying a tray of bowls high on one arm; or the young saleswoman who bows with a gesture so deep, so ritualized that it loses all servility, before the customers of a department store leaving to take an escalator; or the Pachinko player inserting, propelling, and receiving his marbles, with three gestures whose very coordination is a design; or the dandy in the café who with a ritual gesture (abrupt and male) pops open the plastic envelope of his hot napkin with which he will wipe his hands before drinking his Coca-Cola: all these incidents are the very substance of the haiku.

So

The haiku's task is to achieve exemption from meaning within a perfectly readerly discourse (a contradiction denied to Western art, which can contest meaning only by rendering its discourse incomprehensible), so that to our eyes the haiku is neither eccentric nor familiar: it resembles nothing at all: readerly, it seems to us simple, close, known, delectable, delicate, "poetic"—in a word, offered to a whole range of reassuring predicates; insignificant nonetheless, it resists us, finally loses the adjectives which a moment before we had bestowed upon it, and enters into that suspension of meaning which to us is the strangest thing of all, since it makes impossible the most ordinary exercise of our language, which is commentary. What are we to say of this:

Spring breeze:
The boatman chews his grass stem.

or this:

Full moon
And on the matting
The shadow of a pine tree.

or of this:

> *In the fisherman's house*
> *The smell of dried fish*
> *And heat.*

or again (but not finally, for the examples are countless) of this:

> *The winter wind blows.*
> *The cats' eyes*
> *Blink.*

Such *traces* (the word suits the haiku, a kind of faint gash inscribed upon time) establish what we have been able to call "the vision without commentary." This vision (the word is still too Western) is in fact entirely privative; what is abolished is not meaning but any notion of finality: the haiku serves none of the purposes (though they themselves are quite gratuitous) conceded to literature: insignificant (by a technique of meaning-arrest), how could it instruct, express, divert? In the same way, whereas certain Zen schools conceive of seated meditation as a practice *intended* for the obtaining of Buddhahood, others reject even this (apparently essential) finality: one must remain seated *"just to remain seated."* Is not the haiku (like the countless graphic gestures which mark modern and social Japanese life) also written *"just to write"*?

What disappears in the haiku are the two basic functions of our (age-old) classical writing: on the one hand, description (the boatman's grass stem, the pine tree's shadow, the smell of fish, the winter wind are not described, i.e., embellished with significations, with moralities, committed as indices to the revelation of a truth or of a sentiment: meaning is denied to reality; furthermore, reality no longer commands even the meaning of reality); and on the other, definition; not only is definition transferred to gesture, if only a graphic gesture, but it is also shunted toward a kind of inessential—eccentric—efflorescence of the object, as one Zen anecdote puts it nicely, in which the master awards the prize for definition (*what is a fan?*) not even to the silent, purely gestural illustration of function (*to wave the fan*), but to the invention of a chain of aberrant actions (*to close the fan and scratch one's neck with it, to reopen it, put a cookie on it and offer it to the master*). Neither describing nor defining, the haiku (as I shall finally name any discontinuous feature, any event of Japanese life as it offers itself to my reading), the haiku diminishes to the point of pure and sole designation. *It's that, it's thus*, says the haiku, *it's so.* Or better still: *so!* it says, with a touch so instantaneous and so brief (without vibration or recurrence) that even the copula would seem excessive, a kind of remorse for a forbidden, permanently alienated definition. Here meaning is only a flash, a slash of light: *When the light of sense goes out, but with a flash that has revealed the invisible world*, Shakespeare wrote; but the haiku's flash illumines, reveals nothing; it is the flash of a photograph one takes very carefully (in the Japanese manner) but having neglected to load the camera with film. Or again: haiku reproduces the designating gesture of the child pointing at whatever it is (the haiku shows no partiality for the subject), merely saying: *that!* with a movement so immediate (so stripped of any mediation: that of knowledge, of nomination, or even of possession) that what is designated is the very inanity of any classification of the object: *nothing special*, says the haiku, in accordance with the spirit of Zen: the event is not namable according to any species, its specialty short circuits: like a decorative loop, the haiku coils back on itself, the wake of the sign which seems to have been traced is erased: nothing has been acquired, the word's stone has been cast for nothing: neither waves nor flow of meaning.

Stationery Store

It is at the stationery store, site and catalogue of things necessary to writing, that we are introduced into the space of signs; it is in the stationery store that the hand encounters the instrument and the substance of the stroke, the trace, the line, the graphism; it is in the stationery store that the commerce of the sign begins, even before it is written. Hence each nation has its stationery store. That of the United States is abundant, precise, ingenious; it is an emporium for architects, for students, whose commerce must foresee the most relaxed postures; it says that the user experiences no need to invest himself in his writing, but that he must have all the commodities necessary to record in comfort the products of memory, of reading, of teaching, of communication; a good domination of the utensile, but no hallucination of the stroke, of the tool; thrust back into pure applications, writing is never understood as the interplay of a pulsion. The French stationery store, often localized in "*Establishments founded in 18—*," their black marble escutcheons encrusted with gold letters, remains a *papeterie of* bookkeepers, of scribes, of commerce; its exemplary product is the minute, the juridical and calligraphed duplicate, its patrons are the eternal copyists, Bouvard and Pécuchet.

The object of the Japanese stationery store is that ideographic writing which to our eyes seems to derive from painting, whereas quite simply it is painting's inspiration (important that art should have a scriptural and not an expressive origin). To the degree that this Japanese stationery store invents forms and qualities for the two primordial substances of writing, i.e., the surface and the drawing instrument, to the same degree, comparatively, it neglects those byways of registration which form the fantasmal luxury of American establishments: since in Japan the stroke excludes erasure or repetition (since the character is drawn *alla prima*), no invention of the eraser or of its substitutes (the eraser, emblematic object of the signified one wants to erase altogether or whose plenitude, at the very least, one would like to lighten, to reduce; but on the other side of the street, on the Oriental side, why erasers, since the mirror is empty?). Everything, in the instrumentation, is directed toward the paradox of an irreversible and fragile writing, which is simultaneously, contradictorily, incision and glissade; papers of a thousand kinds, many of which hint, in their texture powdered with pale straws, with crushed stems, at their fibrous origin; notebooks whose pages are folded double, like those of a book which has not been cut so that writing moves across a luxury of surfaces and never runs, ignorant of the metonymic impregnation of the right and wrong side of the page (it is traced above a void): palimpsest, the erased stroke which thereby becomes a secret, is impossible. As for the brush (passed across a faintly moistened inkstone), it has its gestures, as if it were the finger; but whereas our old pens knew only clogging or loosening and could only, moreover, scratch the paper always in the same direction, the brush can slide, twist, lift off, the stroke being made, so to speak, in the volume of the air; it has the carnal, lubrified flexibility of the hand. The felt-tipped pen, of Japanese origin, has taken up where the brush leaves off: this stylo is not an improvement of the point, itself a product of the pen (of steel or of cartilage), its immediate ancestry is that of the ideogram. This notion of graphism, to which every Japanese stationery store refers (in each department store, there is a public writer who draws, on long, red-bordered envelopes, the vertical addresses of the gifts), is to be rediscovered, paradoxically (at least as far as we are concerned), even in the typewriter; ours is quick to transform writing into a mercantile product: it pre-edits the text at the very moment one writes it; theirs, by its countless characters, no longer aligned in a single stitching row of letters but rolled on drums, refers to the ideographic marquetry scattered across the sheet—in a word, space; hence the machine extends, at least potentially, a true graphic art which would no longer be the aesthetic labor of the solitary letter but the abolition of the sign, flung aslant, freehand, in all the directions of the page.

The Written Face

The theatrical face is not painted (made up), it is written. There occurs this unforeseen movement: though painting and writing share the same original instrument, the brush, it is still not painting which lures writing into its decorative style, into its flaunted, caressing touch, into its representative space (as would no doubt have been the case with us—in the West the civilized future of a function is always its aesthetic ennoblement); on the contrary, it is the act of writing which subjugates the pictural gesture, so that *to paint* is never anything but *to inscribe*. This theatrical face (masked in No, drawn in Kabuki, artificial in Bunraku) consists of two substances: the white of the paper, the black of the inscription (reserved for the eyes).

The white of the face seems to have as its function, not to denature the flesh tints or to caricature them (as with our clowns, whose white flour and greasepaint are only an incitation to daub the face), but exclusively to erase all anterior trace of the features, to transform the countenance to the blank extent of a matte stuff which no natural substance (flour, paste, plaster, or silk) metaphorically enlivens with a texture, a softness, or a highlight. The face is only: *the thing to write*; but this future is already written by the hand which has whitened the eyelashes, the tip of the nose, the cheekbones, and given the page of flesh its black limit of a wig compact as stone. The whiteness of the face, not lustrous but heavy, as disturbingly dense as sugar, signifies simultaneously two contradictory movements: immobility (for which our "moral" term is: impassivity) and fragility (which in the same fashion but with no more success we label: emotivity). Not *on* this surface but engraved, incised within it, the strictly elongated slit of the eyes and of the mouth. The eyes, barred, unhooped by the straight, flat eyelid, supported by no lower circle (circles under the eyes: a properly expressive value of the Occidental face: fatigue, morbidity, eroticism)—the eyes debouch directly onto the face, as if they were the black and empty source of the writing, "the night of the inkwell"; or again: the face is drawn like a sheet of cloth toward the black (but not "somber") pit of the eyes. Reduced to the elementary signifiers of writing (the blank of the page and the indentations of its script), the face dismisses any signified, i.e., any expressivity: this writing writes nothing (or writes: *nothing*); not only does it not "lend" itself (a naïvely mercantile word) to any emotion, to any meaning (not even that of impassivity, of inexpressiveness), but it actually copies no character whatever: the transvestite actor (since the women's roles are played by men) is not a boy made up as a woman, by dint of a thousand nuances, realistic touches, costly simulations, but a pure signifier whose *underneath* (the truth) is neither clandestine (jealously masked) nor surreptitiously signed (by a waggish wink at the virility of the support, as in Western drag shows: opulent blondes whose trivial hand or huge foot infallibly give the lie to the hormonal bosom): simply *absented*; the actor, in his face, does not play the woman, or copy her, but only signifies her; if, as Mallarmé says, writing consists of "gestures of the idea," transvestism here is the gesture of femininity, not its plagiarism; it follows

89

This Western lecturer, as soon as he is "cited" by the *Kobe Shinbun*, finds himself "Japanned," eyes elongated, pupils blackened by Nipponese typography

遣文化使節として来日した。二十日まで滞在し、その間関東大、京大など数カ所で講演を行なう予定である。しかし、いままティックな著者はフランスの批評家である。

人文科学を駆使バルトの名前は日本ではほとんど知られていない。（処女作「文体＝エクリチュール＝の原点」が森本和夫氏によって「零度の文これまでの著るだろう。前「問題の」批シュレ論」一ー文論」「批「批評と

Whereas the young actor Teturo Tanba, "citing" Anthony Perkins, has lost his Asiatic eyes. What then is our face, if not a "citation"?

that it is not at all remarkable, i.e., not at all marked (a thing inconceivable in the West, where transvestism is already in itself ill conceived and ill supported, purely transgressive), to see an actor of fifty (very famous and much honored) playing the part of a young woman, timorous and in love; for youth—no more than femininity here—is not a natural essence whose truth we madly pursue; the refinement of the code, its precision, indifferent to any extended copy of an organic type (to provoke the real, physical body of a young woman), have as their effect—or justification—to absorb and eliminate all feminine reality in the subtle diffraction of the signifier: signified but not represented, Woman is an idea, not a nature; as such, she is restored to the classifying function and to the truth of her pure difference: the Western transvestite wants to be a (particular) woman, the Oriental actor seeks nothing more than to combine the signs of Woman.

However, insofar as these signs are extreme, not because they are rhetorical (one sees that they are not so), but because they are intellectual—being, like writing, "the gestures of the idea"—they purify the body of all expressivity: one might say that by dint of being signs they extenuate meaning. Which explains that conjunction of sign and impassivity (the word is unsuitable, as noted, because it is moral, expressive) which marks the Asiatic theater. This touches on a certain way of taking death. To imagine, to fabricate a face, not impassive or callous (which is still a meaning), but as though emerged from water, rinsed of meaning, is a way of answering death. Look at this photograph from September 13, 1912: General Nogi, victor over the Russians at Port Arthur, has himself photographed with his wife; their emperor having just died, they have decided to commit suicide the following day; hence, they *know*; he, lost in his beard, his kepi,

They are going to die, they know it,

and this is not seen

his decorations, has almost no face at all; but she reveals hers entire—impassive? stupid? dignified? peasant-like? As in the case of the transvestite actor, no adjective is possible, the predicate is dismissed, not by the solemnity of imminent death, but quite the contrary, by the exemption of Death's meaning, of Death as meaning. General Nogi's wife has decided that Death was the meaning, that she and Death were to be dismissed at the same time, and that therefore, were it to be in her countenance itself, there was to be no "mention" of it.

Millions of Bodies

A Frenchman (unless he is abroad) cannot classify French faces; doubtless he perceives faces in common, but the abstraction of these repeated faces (which is the class to which they belong) escapes him. The body of his compatriots, invisible by its quotidian situation, is a language he can attach to no code; the *déjà vu* of faces has for him no intellectual value; beauty, if he encounters it, is never for him an essence, the summit or the fulfillment of a research, the fruit of an intelligible maturation of the species, but only a piece of luck, a protuberance from platitude, a departure from repetition. Conversely, this same Frenchman, if he sees a Japanese in Paris, perceives him in the pure abstraction of his race (supposing that he does not see him simply as an Asiatic); between these very rare Japanese bodies, he cannot introduce any difference; much more: having unified the Japanese race in a single type, he abusively relates this type to his cultural image of the Japanese, as constructed from not even films, for these films have offered him only anachronistic beings, peasants or samurai, who belong less to "Japan" than to the object "Japanese film," but from a few press photographs, a few newsreel flashes; and this archetypical Japanese is quite lamentable; a skinny creature, wearing glasses, of no specific age, in correct and lusterless clothes, a minor employee of a gregarious country.

In Japan, everything changes: the nothingness or the excess of the exotic code, to which the Frenchman at home is condemned when confronting the *foreigner* (whom he calls *the stranger* though he does not manage to make anything very strange out of him), is absorbed into a new dialectic of speech and language, of series and individual, of body and race (we can speak of dialectic literally, since what arrival in Japan reveals, in a single huge stroke, is the transformation of quality by quantity, of the petty official into exuberant diversity). The discovery is prodigious: streets, shops, bars, cinemas, trains open the huge dictionary of faces and figures in which each body (each word) means only itself and yet refers to a class; hence one has both the pleasure of an encounter (with fragility, with singularity) and the illumination of a type (the feline, the peasant, the apple, the savage, the Lapp, the intellectual, the sleepyhead, the moon-face, the smiler, the dreamer), source of an intellectual jubilation, since the unmasterable is mastered. Immersed in this nation of a hundred million bodies (one will prefer this quantification to that of "souls"), one escapes the double platitude of absolute diversity, which is finally no more than pure repetition (as is the case of the Frenchman at odds with his compatriots), and of the unique class, all difference mutilated (the case of the Japanese petty official as we imagine we see him in Europe). Yet here, as in other semantic groups, the system is valid at its vanishing points: a type imposes itself and yet its individuals are never found side by side; in each population which a public place reveals, analogous in this to the sentence, you grasp singular but known signs, new but potentially repeated bodies; in such a scene, there are never two sleepyheads or two smilers together at the same time, yet one and the other unite with a knowledge: the stereotype is baffled but the intelligible is preserved. Or again —another vanishing point of the code—certain unexpected combinations are discovered: the savage and the feminine coincide, the smooth and the disheveled, the dandy and the student, etc., producing, in the series, new departures, ramifications both distinct and inexhaustible. One might say Japan imposes the same dialectic on its bodies as on its objects: look at the handkerchief shelf in a department store: countless, all different, yet no intolerance in the series, no subversion of order. Or again, the haiku: how many haiku in the history of Japan? They all say the same thing: season, vegetation, sea, village, silhouette, yet each is in its way an irreducible event. Or again, ideographic signs: logically unclassifiable, since they escape an arbitrary but limited, hence memorable, phonetic order (the alphabet), yet classified in dictionaries, where it is—admirable presence of the body in writing and in classification—the number and order of the gestures necessary to draw the ideogram which determine the typology of the signs. And the same for bodies: all Japanese (and not: Asiatics) form a general body (but not a total one, as we assume from our Occidental distance), and yet a vast tribe of different bodies, each of which refers to a class, which vanishes, without disorder, in the direction of an interminable order; in a word: open, to the last moment, like a logical system. The result—or the stake—of this dialectic is the following: the Japanese body achieves the limit of its individuality (like the Zen master when he *invents* a preposterous and upsetting answer to the disciple's serious and banal question), but this individuality cannot be understood in the Western sense; it is pure of all hysteria, does not aim at making the individual into an original body, distinguished from other bodies, inflamed by that promotional fever which

97

infects the West. Here individuality is not closure, theater, outstripping, victory; it is simply difference, refracted, without privilege, from body to body. That is why beauty is not defined here, in the Western manner, by an inaccessible singularity: it is resumed here and there, it runs from difference to difference, arranged in the great syntagm of bodies.

The Eyelid

The several features which compose an ideographic character are drawn in a certain order, arbitrary but regular; the line, beginning with a full brush, ends with a brief point, inflected, turned away at the last moment of its direction. It is this same tracing of a pressure which we rediscover in the Japanese eye. As if the anatomist-calligrapher set his full brush on the inner corner of the eye and, turning it slightly, with a single line, as it must be in painting *alla prima*, opens the face with an elliptical slit which he closes toward the temple with a rapid turn of his hand; the stroke is perfect because simple, immediate, instantaneous, and yet ripe as those circles which it takes a lifetime to learn to make in a single sovereign gesture. The eye is thus contained between the parallels of its lids and the double (inverted) curve of its extremities: it looks like the silhouetted imprint of a leaf, a broad comma painted sideways. The eye is flat (that is its miracle); neither exorbital nor shrunken, without padding, without pouch, and so to speak without skin, it is the smooth slit in a smooth surface. The pupil, intense, fragile, mobile, intelligent (for this eye barred, interrupted by the upper edge of the slit, seems to harbor thereby a reserved pensivity, a dose of intelligence kept in reserve, not *behind* the gaze but *above*)—the pupil is not dramatized by the

Par-dessous la paupière
        de porcelaine,
une large goutte noire :
la Nuit de l'Encrier,
dont parle Mallarmé.

Under the porcelain eyelid,
a broad black drop:
the Night of the Inkwell,
of which Mallarmé speaks.

orbit, as in Western morphology; the eye is free in its slit (which it fills sovereignly and subtly), and it is quite mistakenly (by an obvious ethnocentrism) that we French call it *bridé* (bridled, constrained); nothing restrains the eye, for since it is inscribed at the very level of the skin and not sculptured in the bone structure, its space is that of the entire face. The Western eye is subject to a whole mythology of the soul, central and secret, whose fire, sheltered in the orbital cavity, radiates toward a fleshy, sensuous, passional exterior; but the Japanese face is without moral hierarchy; it is entirely alive, even vivid (contrary to the legend of Oriental hieratism), because its morphology cannot be read "in depth," i.e., according to the axis of an inwardness; its model is not sculptural but scriptural: it is a flexible, fragile, close-woven stuff (silk, of course), simply and as though immediately calligraphed by two lines; "life" is not in the light of the eyes, it is in the non-secret relation of a surface and its slits: in that gap, that difference, that syncope which are, it is said, the open form of pleasure. With so few morphological elements, the descent into sleep (which we can observe on so many faces, in trains and evening subways) remains an easy operation: without a fold of skin, the eye cannot "grow heavy"; it merely traverses the measured degrees of a gradual unity, progressively assumed by the face: eyes lowered, eyes closed, eyes "asleep," a closed line closes further in a lowering of the eyelids which is never ended.

The Writing of Violence

When one says that the *Zengakuren* riots are organized, one refers not only to a group of tactical precautions (incipient notion already contradictory to the myth of the riot) but to a writing of actions which expurgates violence from its Occidental being: spontaneity. In our mythology, violence is caught up in the same prejudice as literature or art: we can attribute to it no other function than that of *expressing* a content, an inwardness, a nature, of which it is the primary, savage, asystematic language; we certainly conceive, no doubt, that violence can be shunted toward deliberated goals, turned into an instrument of thought, but this is never anything but a question of domesticating an *anterior*, sovereignly original force. The violence of the *Zengakuren* does not precede its own regulation, but is born simultaneously with it: it is immediately a sign: expressing nothing (neither hatred nor indignation nor any moral idea), it does away with itself all the more surely in a transitive goal (to besiege and capture a town hall, to open a barbed-wire barrier); yet effectiveness is not its only measurement; a purely pragmatic action puts the symbols between parentheses, but does not settle their account: one utilizes the subject, while leaving it intact (the very situation of the soldier). The *Zengakuren* riot, entirely functional as it is,

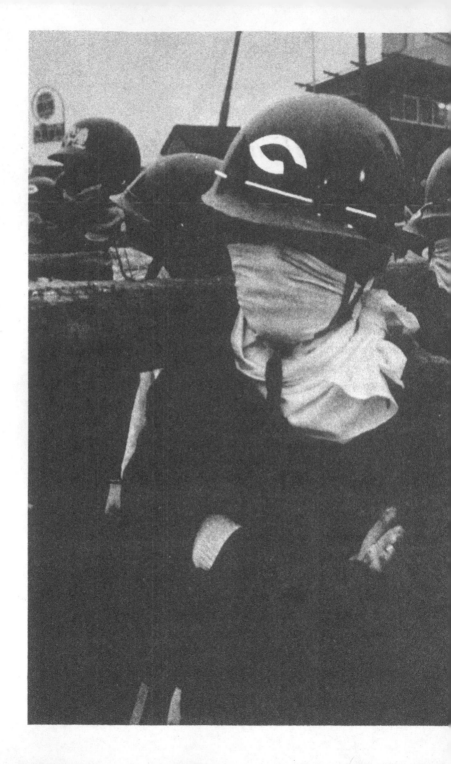

Étudiants

Students

remains a great scenario of signs (these are actions which have a public), the features of this writing, rather more numerous than a phlegmatic, Anglo-Saxon representation of effectiveness would suppose, are indeed discontinuous, arranged, regulated, not in order to signify something but as if to do away (to our eyes) with the myth of the improvised riot, the plenitude of "spontaneous" symbols: there is a paradigm of colors—*red-white-blue helmets*—but these colors, contrary to ours, refer to nothing historical; there is a syntax of actions (*overturn, uproot, drag, pile*), performed like a prosaic sentence, not like an inspired ejaculation; there is a signifying reprise of time-out (leaving in order to rest behind the lines, giving a form to relaxation). All this combines to produce a mass writing, not a group writing (the gestures are completed, the persons do not assist each other); finally, the extreme risk of the sign, it is sometimes acknowledged that the slogans chanted by the combatants should utter not the Cause, the Subject of the action (what one is fighting for or against)—this would be once again to make language the expression of a reason, the assurance of a good cause—but only this action itself (*The* Zengakuren *are going to fight*), which is thereby no longer covered, directed, justified, made innocent by language—that external divinity superior to the combat, like a Marseillaise in her Phrygian bonnet—but doubled by a pure vocal exercise which simply adds to the volume of violence, a gesture, one muscle more.

The Cabinet of Signs

In any and every site of this country, there occurs a special organization of space: traveling (in the street, in trains through the suburbs, over the mountains), I perceive the conjunction of a distance and a division, the juxtaposition of fields (in the rural and visual sense) simultaneously discontinuous and open (patches of tea plantations, of pines, of mauve flowers, a composition of black roofs, a grillwork of alleyways, a dissymmetrical arrangement of low houses): no enclosure (except for very low ones) and yet I am never besieged by the horizon (and its whiff of dreams): no craving to swell the lungs, to puff up the chest to make sure of my ego, to constitute myself as the assimilating center of the infinite: brought to the evidence of an empty limit, I am limitless without the notion of grandeur, without a metaphysical reference.

From the slope of the mountains to the neighborhood intersection, here everything is habitat, and I am always in the most luxurious room of this habitat: this luxury (which is elsewhere that of the kiosks, of corridors, of fanciful structures, collectors' cabinets, of private libraries) is created by the fact that the place has no other limit than its carpet of living sensations, of brilliant signs (flowers, windows, foliage, pictures, books); it is no longer the great continuous wall which defines space, but the very abstraction of the fragments of view (of the "views") which frame me; the wall is destroyed beneath the inscription; the garden is a mineral tapestry of tiny volumes (stones, traces of the rake on the sand), the public place is a series of instantaneous events which accede to the notable in a flash so vivid, so tenuous that the sign does away with itself before any particular signified has had the time to "take." One might say that an age-old technique permits the landscape or the spectacle to produce itself, to occur in a pure significance, abrupt, empty, like a fracture. Empire of Signs? Yes, if it is understood that these signs are empty and that the ritual is without a god. Look at the cabinet of Signs (which was the Mallarmean habitat), i.e., in that country, any view, urban, domestic, rural, and the better to see how it is made, take for example the Shikidai gallery: tapestried with openings, framed with emptiness and framing nothing, decorated no doubt, but so that the figuration (flowers, trees, birds, animals) is removed, sublimated, displaced far from the foreground of the view, there is in it place for furniture (a paradoxical word in French—*meuble* —since it generally designates a property anything but mobile, concerning which one does everything so that it will endure: with us, furniture has an immobilizing vocation, whereas in Japan the house, often deconstructed, is scarcely more than a furnishing—mobile—element); in the Shikidai gallery, as in the ideal Japanese house, stripped of furniture (or scantily furnished), there is no site which designates the slightest propriety in the strict sense of the word—ownership: neither seat nor bed nor table out of which the body might

Close to smiling

108

constitute itself as the subject (or master) of a space: the center is rejected (painful frustration for Western man, everywhere "furnished" with his armchair, his bed, proprietor of a domestic *location*). Uncentered, space is also reversible: you can turn the Shikidai gallery upside down and nothing would happen, except an inconsequential inversion of top and bottom, of right and left: the content is irretrievably dismissed: whether we pass by, cross it, or sit down on the floor (or the ceiling, if you reverse the image), there is nothing to *grasp*.